Peace Education and the Adult Learner

Educational Trends in a Globalized World

Jason J. Campbell and
Noël E. Campbell

UNIVERSITY PRESS OF AMERICA,® INC.
Lanham • Boulder • New York • Toronto • Plymouth, UK

Copyright © 2012 by
University Press of America,® Inc.
4501 Forbes Boulevard
Suite 200
Lanham, Maryland 20706
UPA Acquisitions Department (301) 459-3366

Estover Road
Plymouth PL6 7PY
United Kingdom

All rights reserved
Printed in the United States of America
British Library Cataloging in Publication Information Available

Library of Congress Control Number: 2011935690
ISBN: 978-0-7618-5677-1 (paperback : alk. paper)
eISBN: 978-0-7618-5678-8

∞™ The paper used in this publication meets the minimum
requirements of American National Standard for Information
Sciences—Permanence of Paper for Printed Library Materials,
ANSI Z39.48-1992

Contents

1	The Andragogy of Peace	1
2	Globalization and the Adult Learner	39
3	Peace Education and International Diplomacy	47
4	Kantian Cosmopolitism and a League of Nations	63
References		87

Chapter One

The Andragogy of Peace

Peacekeepers, peacemakers and international negotiators face a daunting task in the global resolution of 21st century conflict. For adult learners interested in peace education and conflict resolution, new andragogical models of teaching peace education will facilitate their self-directed learning. The foundation of these andragogical models must be situated within a discourse of conflict escalation and effective methods for conflict resolution. Teaching adult learners about peace education requires the cultivation of keen critical thinking skills and an understanding of basic conflict resolution strategies. Equipped with these tools, adult learners will invariably develop organic models of conflict resolution. Thus, rather than structuring a formulaic, process-based strategy of peace education, we will simply progress through the andragogy of peace education by analyzing contemporary conflicts and contemplating possible strategies for resolution. It is then, the responsibility of the adult learner to gain the confidence to develop specifically context-based resolution strategies, rather than broadly apply generalized theoretical models to very specific instances of conflict.

GLOBALIZATION AND PEACEKEEPING

In a contemporary analysis of international conflict, adult learners must understand the complexities of collective action and peacekeeping. They must recognize the difficult nuances of collective action and begin to formulate context-based resolution strategies, rather than trying to apply an abstracted theoretical model to a specific instance of conflict. For example, the escalation of threats to international security, forces intuitions like the United Nations (UN) to "analyze the extraordinary recent evolution of threats to international security and identify [clear contributions] that collective action can make."[1] In an attempt to discuss peace education and the adult learner, learners must first acknowledge the effects of globalization and the difficulties of combating both intra-state violence and threats to international security. As the world becomes increasingly globalized, the destabilization of national security undermines the broader nexus of international security forces. If national security can be destabilized, and since globalization increases the interdependence between nations, the destabilization of national security threatens to undermine interdependency between states. Thus, adult learners should recognize that the demarcation between national sovereignty and a globalized international community is becoming increasingly blurred.

This line has, in part, been blurred because of the increasing economic interdependency between nations. In fact, it may be argued that globalization has directly facilitated in the growing economic interdependency between states. For example, in a 2011 report on the effects of globalization and China's membership in the World Trade Organization (WTO), Director-General

Pascal Lamy noted, "I don't think there is any question that China joining the WTO has been a very good thing for China and for the WTO and its members . . . in joining the WTO, China successfully underpinned a policy of what had been 20 years of *progressive openness* (emphasis added)."[2]

This notion of being progressively open to both change, especially technological change, and a rapidly changing economic landscape, fosters sociocultural and economic interdependency between states. It is at least plausible to suggest that the more socially, economically, and culturally interdependent individual nations are, the greater the likelihood that they will attempt to preserve peace between their respective nations. Even if such actions are motivated by the economic benefits afforded from stabilized peace, at least peace is stabilized. Thus, globalization can and does serve as a conduit for creating economic and cultural opportunities between states, which would otherwise not exist. For the adult learner interested in becoming a peacekeeper, the increased interdependency between states can facilitate the preservation of peace and diplomacy, because peaceful relations between states are a necessary condition for healthy and sustainable economic markets. There can be then, infinitely many strategies to develop this global interdependency. In defense of the economic benefits that globalization has had, Swaminathan Aiyar states,

> the notion that India is being subjugated is nonsense . . . Globalisation creates on a global scale opportunities that were earlier available only *within nations* . . . Globalisation is unstoppable because it is based not on western domination . . . *China is the best example of using globalisation for economic success. Far from becoming a western puppet, it now challenges western supremacy* (emphasis added).[3]

While there are certainly disadvantages to increased globalization, there are also many benefits. Globalization, as noted in the preceding quote, is not based on Western domination. The spread of globalization has empowered developing nations and substantially increased the standard of living for many throughout the developing world. In fact, the redistribution of global wealth has forced many Western laborers to recognize that they must now compete with laborers on a global scale. Far from being a mechanism of enforcing Western domination, globalization challenges Western domination by allowing global access to the economic benefits of embracing globalized markets. The more these markets are embraced, the greater the distribution of wealth. Securing and safeguarding the economic integrity of these markets must begin with a recognition that interstate peace contributes to stabilization.

For the adult learner then, developing and refining context-based methods of stabilizing economic markets, empowers them to adapt and modify their respective approaches to the process of stabilizing peace. Thus, rather than arbitrarily creating a series of steps wherein regional stability is attained, we believe that simply recognizing this relationship will allow adult learners to create their own context-based approaches to regional stabilization. Since regional stabilization takes place within the broader context of globalization, and since regional stabilization is contingent on the economic stability of local markets, a context-specific understanding of local markets aids in the broader understanding of globalization. Thus, adult learners must recognize that for states to preserve these continual streams of capital, peaceful relations and a growing interdependency between states must function as a necessary condition for maintaining regional peace, i.e., an influx of economic capital, as a consequence of globalization, is itself contingent on peaceful relations between states. The economic benefits of globalization that are reciprocated between states must serve as an incentive to maintain and stabilize peace. Thus, achieving peace will depend on the ability to stabilize regional economic markets.

We are not idealists. We recognize that the motivation for international cooperation between states is potentially only viable insofar as there is money to be made, which unfortunately suggests that states outside the nexus of trade and economic exchange can and most likely will be exploited as a means of maximizing capital gains. Unfortunately, exploitation is a negative consequence of capitalism. More than any other country, the collected countries within Africa face the greatest threat of economic and resource exploitation. The responsibility to protect vulnerable populations throughout the many countries of Africa becomes the responsibility of their respective leaders. Thus, "African governments must ensure that infrastructure development does not just support the exploitation and export of minerals but also facilitates trade and the movement of people and goods. Local workforces must be trained in new skills and not just used for manual labour."[4]

Within the 21st century, governmental nonparticipation in globalized markets is tantamount to the economic destruction of the state. States must function within the context of a globalized world. Though these markets, like all markets, lend themselves to abuse and economic exploitation, it is not being suggested that exploitation is an inherent or subsistent aspect of globalization, since both developing countries and superpowers have benefited from a globalized world economy. Peacekeeping and conflict resolution, at the international level, are simply good business practices. Adult learners can offer meaningful contributions to international peacekeeping efforts by globalizing their educational experience.

The preservation of peace and the resolution of international conflict, in-and-of-itself, may prove ill-suited to resolve the major conflicts that arise as a natural consequence of globalized economies. The moral assertions which apply to individual moral agents, have consistently failed to motivate states to act in accordance with complex moral laws. The truth is, not all states are motivated to protect their respective populations, as evident in acts of genocide. Not all states are egalitarian in the distribution of power. Unequivocally, however, all states need capital to survive. Thus, if the survival of the state is contingent on capital, and the most effective means of gaining an influx of capital is through globalization, which exists through the interdependency between states, then preserving peace between states strengthens this interdependency. Furthermore, the preservation of peace between states stabilizes economic markets, thereby serving the interests of each state. Peace can be profitable. Thus, recognizing the profitability of peace is of utmost importance for adult learners and their attempts to pacify escalating international conflict.

CONSUMER CONFIDENCE AND GLOBAL PEACE

Where interdependency is strengthened, connected states stand to gain economic benefit. Preserving this relationship, however, will require new modes of collective and cooperative action between states and new modes of stabilizing economic markets, especially after the global recession of 2008. It is likely that the International Monetary Fund (IMF) must assume a new operational structure to secure these markets, because instability within the market will surely result in the destabilization of international peace.

> To accommodate the needs of the emerging economies, as well as the interests of advanced countries, *a new system will be needed*, in which exchange rates are managed but adjusted according to criteria that balance domestic growth and global stability. The IMF will be at the center of the design and implementation of any new system, by reason of mandate and expertise (emphasis added).[5]

The development of new and emerging economies introduces new business partners into the broader nexus of globalization. Insofar as new connections are made, new possibilities to spread and safeguard peaceful business relations must result in new attempt to secure diplomacy between states. Securing diplomacy can only result from the efforts of highly trained adult learners educated in the andragogy of peace. Thus within the coming decade, educators must develop and formalize an andragogy of peace. The emergence of this field can only develop from the collaborative efforts of interdisciplinary educators, the world over.

There is then, an intimate connection between peacekeeping, on the one hand, and both economic stability and consumer confidence, on the other. The restoration of consumer confidence in the stability of markets directly impacts the stabilization of peace across diverse regions. For example, it has been stated that, "the global economic crisis has shown that multilateralism matters. Staring into the abyss, *countries pulled together to save the global economy*. The modern G-20 was borne out of crisis. It showed its potential by quickly acting to shore up confidence" (emphasis added).[6] Multilateralism is itself strengthened by globalized markets. The collective and cooperative action to "save the global economy" was motivated by the recognition of economic interdependency between states. Money is an undeniable motivator to foster cooperative action. Thus, adult learners must recognize that preserving and safeguarding the economic viability of global markets motivated such cooperation; peacebuilders can operationalize this motivation by demonstrating that the market is itself contingent on the stabilization of peace. Learners must acknowledge the correlation between interstate dependency and the stabilization of international peace if they are to become effective peacebuilders.

Consumer confidence in stabilized economic markets influences state interdependency. Preserving economic interdependency promotes interstate peace. Thus, if consumer confidence influences interdependency, and if interdependency promotes peace, then consumer confidence can serve as a tool to promote peace. As the nexus of economic interdependency between states increase, interstate conflict should decrease. The decrease of interstate conflict should follow as a direct result of self interest. Thus, it is in the best interest of any state to minimize interstate conflict. In fact, in the case of Iraq, for example, the IMF has warned that "a prolonged war in Iraq could depress financial markets and put global economic recovery in jeopardy . . . *the longer the conflict persisted, the more pessimistic investors would be*" (emphasis added).[7]

It is difficult if not impossible for investors to have confidence in financial markets where conflict is prevalent. Conflict is counterproductive. In short, conflict is bad for business. Investor pessimism can economically cripple already conflict ridden regions. The presence of conflict essentially removes confidence from the market, which results in a very slippery slope. If conflict destabilizes financial markets, and if the destabilization of financial markets results in more conflict, then it is easy to understand how destabilized financial markets breed conflict. It is also easy to understand how conflict suffocates economic progress. Conversely, however, the stabilization of peace benefits financial markets by giving potential investors the confidence necessary to invest in the market. Thus, peace serves as a necessary though not sufficient condition to promote investor confidence.

In discussing the escalating conflict in Sudan, the relationship between investor confidence and the stabilization of regional peace was directly addressed.

> A report by Frontier Economics Limited . . . warned that such a conflict could have devastating economic consequences. "This report demonstrates the high cost of conflict," said Matthew Bell, Associate Director of the London-based Frontier Economics . . . Sudan's neighbours, such as Kenya and Ethiopia, would also lose up to 25 billion dollars as their economies suffered *due to decreased investor confidence in the region* . . . (emphasis added).[8]

The stabilization of peace throughout zones of conflict clearly contributes to an increase in investor confidence. The "high cost of conflict" undermines this confidence and further destabilizes the region. Thus, adult learners and peacekeepers must recognize the potential economic benefits of promoting peace in zones of conflict and defend peace and conflict resolution as fundamentally important in the viability of local and regional economic markets. There is then, a direct economic benefit in the stabilization of peace. Peace is profitable. Gartzke and Li address the relationship between peace and economic stability:

> the interaction of states and markets is capable of providing positive political externalities. Increasingly, economic agents in

global markets affect bargaining among states by making threats of disruptive conflict costly for political competitors. Because markets respond to risk, political demands coincide with an economic price tag and hence political talk is no longer cheap. *States that are integrated into the global economy are more often able to reveal resolve through their statements and through the associated market responses, rather than through military acts*" (emphasis added).[9]

Peacekeepers must be educated to recognize that the resolution of international conflict and the de-escalation of military force take place within the broader system of international globalized markets. The resolution of international conflict is itself rooted in attempts to maintain economic interdependency between states. Since the economic interdependency between states has been shown to stabilize peace, and since peace has been shown as a necessary though not sufficient condition for the promotion of investor confidence, the greater the economic interdependence between states, the more willing foreign investors will be to invest in these markets. Equipped with this knowledge, adult learners have a new tool in de-escalating military and armed conflict by reminding respective parties of the economic consequence of conflict and the economic benefits of peace.

INTRA-STATE CONFLICT AND PEACEBUILDING

According to the Correlates of War (COW) Project, intra-state war has been subdivided into three types, "based on the status of the combatants: civil wars involve the government of the state against a non-state entity; regional internal wars involve the government of a regional subunit against a non-state entity;

and intercommunal wars involve combat between/among two or more non-state entities within the state."[10]

With the rise of inter-state conflict in Afghanistan, Somalia, Bahrain, Sudan, and the Democratic Republic of the Congo, to name but a few, intra-state conflict has the potential to disrupt regional economic stability, and therefore global economic markets. As noted earlier, the disruption of global economic markets, in general, and regional markets, in particular, adversely affect the stabilization of peace. Thus, there is a very real threat that intra-state conflict can and does have the potential to propagate violence beyond state borders, i.e., intra-state conflict can influence the spread of interstate conflict. In their 2011 article for the *Washington Post*, Thomas Erdbrink and Liz Sly note, "Violent protests erupted in Iran, Yemen and Bahrain on Monday [February 14, 2011] as the revolutionary fervor unleashed by the toppling of Egyptian President Hosni Mubarak rippled across the Middle East, propelling people onto the streets to demand change from a spectrum of autocratic regimes."[11] The destabilization of these autocratic regimes has been largely motivated by the economic disparities between the ruling elite and members of an impoverished population. Thus, as is evident in the Egyptian uprising, the economic exploitation of the people only fuels intra-state conflict, which often spreads throughout the region, thereby destabilizing peacekeeping efforts. Furthermore, it is alleged that the uprising may have itself been initiated by young adults networked through various social media. Though the Egyptian protests were largely peaceful, "The protest in Yemen's capital, Sanaa, on Monday [February 14, 2011] was less well attended, *but also more violent*, than others in the city in recent weeks, highlighting *the potential for instability in a nation already reeling from internal conflicts*, massive poverty and a resurgent branch of al-Qaida" (emphasis added).[12] Internal conflict, by definition, is at the heart of intra-state conflict. As mentioned earlier, this conflict can manifest in a variety of ways. The manner in which conflict emerges, however, is not of particular importance. Nonetheless, of great importance is the existence of intra-state conflict and the potential threat such conflict poses to the stabilization of state sovereignty. The difficulty that intra-state conflict poses to the stabilization of the sate unfolds, as a direct consequence of intercommunal conflict. However, the mere categorization of intra-state conflict, in-and-of-itself, is not sufficient for understanding the nature of the intra-state conflict since at least one aspect of intra-state conflict may directly involve the state as an active party to the conflict. As described in the COW project, "civil wars involve the government of the state against a non-state entity." Thus, the precise nature of this relationship is only recognized in terms of governmental participation. In part, governmental participation in the oppression of the youth led to a domino effect, wherein various rebellions led to regional destabilization. The cooperative effort to destabilize an entire region would be impossible without the global exchange of information via social media. Thus, adult learner must learn to harness this power of digital-interconnectedness.

Intra-state conflict has been described by researchers as a new form of "postmodern conflict" or the "new war" (Kaldor 1999; Duffield 1998).[13] In a post-Cold War era, intra-state conflict has directly resulted in the willful extermination of millions of lives. Ethnic diversity, perceived religious incompatibility, and racial supremacy have served as some of the key intercommunal conflicts, which destabilize intra-state security. Clearly then, these forms of inter-state conflict require comprehensive governmental interaction and engagement, which is not however to suggest that only governmental participation in intra-state conflict exists as the only means of exacerbating the conflict.

PEACEKEEPING, FAILED STATES AND A CATCH 22

The Program on Intrastate Conflict at the Belfer Center for Science and International Affairs at Harvard's Kennedy School of Government defines its intent as: "provid[ing] both practical and conceptual understanding to practitioners and scholars, and also to advance the field of conflict prevention and conflict avoidance by reaching testable propositions about vulnerable states."[14] The success of conflict prevention is contingent on continually assessing the effectiveness of both practical and conceptual approaches to the resolution and prevention of intra-state conflict. The conceptual difficulty in analyzing and discussing intra-state conflict, however, unfolds in the attempt to recognize national sovereignty. If, during an instance of intra-state conflict, national sovereignty is acknowledge, its acknowledgment comes at the expense of intervening and deescalating the conflict. If, however, primacy is placed on intervening in the conflict, intervention comes at the expense of acknowledging national sovereignty. Thus, to acknowledge national sovereignty is to fail to intervene in the conflict; however, to acknowledge intercommunal conflict, is to disregard national sovereignty. The Catch 22 unfolds as a complication of dual recognition. It is difficult, if not impossible, to both acknowledge the sovereignty of the state and also intervene in the conflict. The recognition of one is the denial of the other. Moreover, the issue of recognition is further complicated by governmental participation in the ensuing conflict, as is evident in the case of civil wars and acts of state endorsed genocide. In these instances, governmental participation within the conflict precludes external third party intervention. If third parties recognize that the government is directly involved in the conflict, and these parties are bound to acknowledge state sovereignty, then it is impossible for them to intervene in the conflict despite knowing that the government is directly involved in the conflict. To intervene in the conflict would be to discredit their sovereignty and engage in an act of interstate war. Thus, it is far more difficult for sovereign nations to engage in the immediate resolution of intra-state conflict, where governmental participation has been confirmed. The most effective means of such engagement typically occurs as a consequence of North Atlantic Treaty Organization (NATO) forces and Non-Governmental Organizations, (NGOs). Quite obviously, NATO intervention is limited by its alliances, which suggests that NGO forces could be an effective means of de-escalating intercommunal conflict in failed or failing states. The role that NGOs can play in this direct form of conflict prevention has yet to be seen. Nevertheless, any third party intervention will require recognition of national sovereignty, which inherently limits the effectiveness of any NGO, since the sovereign typifies state authority. There is, however, the possibility that NGO representatives, equipped with an intimate understanding of peacekeeping methods, and culturally sensitive to the plight of targeted members of the population, can gain access to the critical consciousness of their oppression. This recognition, as evident in the recent upsurge in revolts throughout North Africa, is the force behind transformative social change.

Sovereignty then, unfolds as an "authority relationship" (Lake 2003).[15] Within the relationship between those subject to such authority and those in control of the implements of power, sovereignty is often understood in terms of supreme control within the territorial confines of the state. Thus, yielding to the power of the state is mandated by recognizing and acknowledging state sovereignty. It is precisely in this recognition, however, that intra-state humanitarian concerns become international concerns, because there is an ethical obligation to intervene on behalf of those that are either systematically targeted for extermination, as is the case in acts of genocide, or those that are caught in vicious religious, tribal, and ethnical intercommunal conflicts. Insofar as the nature of the conflict is localized within the community, and that community within the larger purview of national sovereignty, the escalation of intercommunal conflict, even to genocidal levels, complicates humanitarian intervention precisely because intervention becomes the responsibility of the state. Thus, the "conceptual understanding" of intra-state conflict is only meaningful within a broader understanding of the difficulty of dual recognition. If the state is not a party to the conflict, as may be the case in small tribal or regional conflict, third party intervention will not be limited by state involvement. Thus, there are better chances of resolving or preventing intercommunal conflict that do not involve governmental participation. Since the government is not involved in such conflict, third party intervention does not threaten state sovereignty. If, however, the government is involved in an act of intra-state conflict, as is the case in acts of civil war or genocide, third party intervention will be complicated by governmental participation. Peacekeeping efforts to resolve intra-state conflict is only viable, then, insofar as there is a clear understanding of these levels of governmental participation. Rival parties to the existing party will encourage governmental participation in the conflict, since those in power will seek to maintain their power and thwart any legitimate attempts at sovereignty.

Thus, in vying for power, political opposition threatens the sovereignty of the state. Insofar as there is a concerted effort to protect the status quo, either military or militia forces are often used to "defend" national sovereignty against outside forces. In the escalating conflict in Libya, for example, Moammar Gadhafi "vowed in a televised speech to cling to power with the last drop of blood" and to "cleanse Libya house by house" or "die here as a martyr trying."[16] This notion of "cleansing" the state indicates the escalation of threat directed against his opposition, threats which all too often result in the systematic extermination of human life. Peacekeepers face a daunting task once the nature of the conflict escalates to this level. Genocidal speech or the intent to "cleanse" the population of all those who oppose political power necessitates the presence of armed peacekeeping forces. It is, then, foolish to disregard the threat of cleansing as of little consequence. Harff and Gurr (1998) discuss the relationship between the notion of cleansing and genocide, "The use of force to cleanse an area of a particular ethnic group . . . is a more extreme example. If 'cleansing' involves widespread killings, the policy is more accurately called genocide."[17] It is easy then to understand how the escalation of intercommunal violence or state-endorsed intrastate violence escalates to the point of genocide. Preventing the escalation of intercommunal conflict, however, especially from peacekeeping forces outside the community is a difficult task indeed. The task of preventing the occurrence of such atrocities rests in the ability of adult learners and peacekeepers to recognize that a policy of wholesale extermination is at least being conceptualized, which is certainly the case in Libya. For Gadhafi to directly assert that he will, "cleanse Libya house by house" suggests that this act of cleansing will unfold from a genocidal policy of extermination. The attempt to prevent the escalation of intra-state conflict to the levels of genocide acts requires peacebuilders and peacekeepers to seriously consider threats of violence. If, for example, after such remarks, members of potentially targeted populations are evacuated from their homes, it is likely that countless lives will be saved by the proactive efforts of well informed peacekeepers. For example, realizing the significance of the threat is actually quite easy. Ashish Kumar Sen, in quoting Secretary of State Hillary Rodham Clinton writes,

> The world is watching the situation in Libya with alarm . . . We join the international community in strongly condemning the violence in Libya. Now is the time to stop this unacceptable bloodshed. Our thoughts and prayers are with those whose lives have been lost, and with their loved ones." The State Department ordered the evacuation of families and nonessential staff from the U.S. Embassy in Tripoli.[18]

Peacekeepers must recognize that the failure of a state serves as an indication of the inevitable transference of power from the status quo to the newly empowered opposition. State failure is the final mode existence for a state that will soon be replaced by its opposition. It is during this transference of power that state officials are most likely to defend their power by resorting to violence.

The escalation of intercommunal conflict, which threatens to undermine state sovereignty, poses a potential threat to the economic stability and security of the state. For peacekeepers to prevent the escalation of conflict within failing states, they must recognize that a weakened state is a vulnerable state. The more intercommunal conflict escalates, the greater threat it poses to overall security. The more this intercommunal conflict jeopardizes state sovereignty, the more vulnerable the state is to internal or external attack.

THREE CHALLENGES TO INTERNATIONAL PEACEBUILDING

Because our world is increasingly globalized, attempts to bolster peace within zones of conflict must be informed by the shared responsibility of collective international action. For example, Ban Ki-moon, Secretary-General of the United Nations recently stated:

> Today, the world is struggling with three major, interlinked crises: the global food crisis; climate change crisis; and a development crisis . . . We can succeed in confronting these problems *only if we act globally, with a common understanding*, bringing together all key players: Governments, donors, international and regional organizations, non-governmental organizations, the private sector and academia (emphasis added).[19]

These three interlinked crises: the global food shortage, climate change, and the development crisis, require a shared understanding and recognition that international cooperation and participation is a fundamental condition for the stabilization of national peace and security. If, in this globalized world, national peace and security are destabilized, it is likely that international peace and security will be compromised.

It was recently noted that, "a confluence of worst-case events beyond the ability of the Yemeni government to control—could lead to a further erosion of central government authority in Yemen and destabilization of the region."[20] Mike Huckabee addressed the potential rippling effect the destabilization of the Egyptian government could have throughout both the region and the world: "The events of the past few days in Egypt have created a very tenuous situation, not just for Egypt, not just for the Middle East, but for the entire world, and the destabilization of that nation has the potential of cascading across the globe."[21] Thus, it is in the interest of each sovereign nation to participate in the international resolution of conflict and crisis management, by attempting to stabilize national peace and security, because as our world becomes increasingly globalized, the preservation of national security will increasingly require stabilized peace throughout the international world. A discourse then, on international peacekeeping strategies must address the role of national peacekeeping since the interdependency of states is itself contingent on the integrity of national security. Since effective intrastate peacekeeping has the potential to influence interstate diplomacy, weaknesses in international peacekeeping, may reflect local or even systemic weakness among interdependent states. Furthermore, since the global food shortage, climate change, and the development crisis are impending systemic crises that threaten international peace, and since international peace is in part contingent on the stabilization of regional and national security, the three crises threatening international peace also pose a serious threat to the individual national security of any given state.

THE GLOBAL FOOD CRISIS AND CLIMATE CHANGE

In addressing these three challenges to the stabilization of international peace and security, it is essential that adult learners recognize the ultimate importance each of these potential hazards play in compromising both peace and security. For example, the 2007 global food crisis drove the international demand to disastrous levels and the prices for consumption crops dramatically increased. The Uzbekistani government and "stakeholders in Tashkent" are currently in collaborative talks with the United Nations Development Program (UNDP) and the World Health Organization (WHO) to optimize food security.[22] There is a cyclical threat to global food security, insofar as the escalating problem of climate change is adversely affecting both cash and consumption crops. Thus, there is a direct correlation between the increase of carbon emissions, the gradual warming of the earth, and the threat it poses to global food security. As, CO_2 emissions increase, the planet becomes increasingly warm. As the planet becomes increasingly warm, the likelihood of mass regional drought spreads. As drought spreads, more people will starve and as more people compete over limited food resources, the likelihood of wide scale violence increases.

As global food security is compromised, populations will increasingly become more violent. "Hon. Athumani Janguo . . . while making a presentation at the Pan African Parliament (PAP) over the global food crisis . . . said Africa was most at risk in the worsening global food situation. The crisis is likely to worsen malnutrition and HIV/AIDS as well as increase crime and violence in Africa."[23] The global increase in violence is itself a product of the decrease in consumption crops and the increase of international prices, which results from the increase of CO_2 emissions. There is a direct relationship between the destabilization of international peace and security and the increase of CO_2 emissions and global warming. The two concepts seem entirely unrelated, but as argued, there is a direct and identifiable connection between global warming and the destabilization of international peace and security. Granted, correlation is never a demonstration of proof, but it is imperative that lawmakers and international humanitarians consider all possible complications to their attempts to maintain international peace. Thus, global warming is both a national and international security issue.

With respect to the climate change crisis and threats to global food security, Tinker (1997) notes,

> The potential interaction between climate change and agriculture may be important and complicated, and the 'global change' and the 'food security' scientific communities need to become even better integrated than now. *It is to be hoped that any food crisis had been overcome before any climate change crisis develops* (emphasis added).[24]

This point should not be taken lightly. It is imperative to recognize the order in which we must attempt to resolve the impending three crises we face in the 21st century. First, global interventionists must attempt to stabilize the global food security crisis before global warming intensifies. If the global food security crisis continues to escalate with an increased escalation of CO_2 emissions and global warming, then the global food crisis can only worsen. The global food crisis is itself a threat to many developing nations throughout the world, and countless lives are lost each year to starvation. Thus, the increase of CO_2 emissions can only exacerbate the global food crisis. If, however, the global food crisis can be stabilized through new innovations in drought resistant crops and better techniques in crop rotation and the preservation of soil integrity, then we can at least suppress the disastrous impact of global food shortages that the intensification of global warming will invariably have. Moreover, since we have previously recognized that there is a direct correlation between the intensification of global warming and the escalation of international violence, new technologies and agricultural advances could indirectly affect the levels of global peace and security. Thus, money and time should be spent developing and improving agricultural technologies, because the research at least suggests that there is a connection between the stabilization of global food supplies and the preservation of international peace and security. The more people have to eat, the less likely they are to resort to violence.

If significant money could be appropriated to the increased development of alternative farming technologies, namely, drought resistant crops and biogenetically engineered foods, the threat of the global food crisis would be limited by these new and alternative methods to stabilize food and consumption crops. Preserving the integrity of fragile consumption crops, through these advances in science and technology, would also contribute to the stabilization of national and regional peace throughout most of the developing world, by ensuring that their respective population had enough to eat. Granted, it is not being suggested that a global economic investment into alternative farming technologies will directly contribute to the stabilization of regional and international peace, but it is certainly plausible.

THE DEVELOPMENT CRISIS

Of the three impending crises that affront the new millennium, the development crises is arguably the least understood and most underestimated. In his remarks to the Millennium Development Goals Summit at the United Nations, President Barack Obama noted:

> in the Universal Declaration of Human Rights, we recognized the inherent dignity and rights of every individual, including the right to a decent standard of living . . . When a child dies from a preventable disease, it shocks all of our consciences. When a girl is deprived of an education or her mother is denied equal rights, it undermines the prosperity of their nation. When a young entrepreneur can't start a new business, it stymies the creation of new jobs and markets in that entrepreneur's country, but also in our own. *When millions of fathers cannot provide for their families, it feeds the despair that can fuel instability and violent extremism.* When a disease goes unchecked, it can endanger the health of millions around the world (emphasis added).[25]

The difficulty in tackling the development crisis is complicated by the inherent conflict embedded in the notion of a right to a decent standard of living. The objector may argue that suppositions of maintaining a decent standard of living, itself presuppose a global welfare system, wherein the haves are forced to contribute to the have-nots. The threat of the development crisis is rooted in both economic and social oppressions, which stymie an acknowledgment of systemic and systematic poverty. What is beyond debate, however, is the relationship between an inability to provide for one's family and the "despair that can fuel instability and violent extremism." Violence becomes an inevitable consequence of poverty once our primal need to eat and to provide basic sustenance for our loved ones cannot be met. Ensuring that (1) there is enough food available for consumption and (2) laborers have the economic means of purchasing this food and providing for themselves and their families is precisely the manner in which we thwart the likelihood of increased violence as a consequence of malnutrition and poverty. The suggestion that a decent standard of living is relative, that it cannot be empirically justified, fails to recognize the pervasive and dehumanizing effects of global poverty.

The basic standard of living is a standard which allows one such provision. It is a standard in which laborers are at least afforded the ability to sustain their own lives. Access to clean drinking water, educational opportunities, and economic possibilities are basic rights every human being must have. Our respective governments are responsible to ensure the provision of these basic rights. Where our governments fail to secure these rights, the population of citizens subject to such a government is morally obligated to revolt. This is of course assuming the primacy of a biological basis in self preservation. If, as biological organisms, we hold self preservation as endemic to the human condition, then it must be the case that our political systems of governance address and satisfy this essential facet of our biology. The development crisis will be the most difficult to counteract simply because its objective basis is less clearly defined than either the global food crisis or even climate change. The development crisis requires more than simply an infusion of global capital into failing economies. It requires more than bailing-out failed institutions. It even requires more than attempts to stabilize the global economy. Counteracting the negative effects of the development crisis requires a wholly new interpretative and theoretical model for human cooperation. It requires that we assume the responsibility of eliminating the distinction between the haves and the have-nots, and we make a sincere effort to humanize the millions of people throughout the world that have systematically been targeted for dehumanization.

COMPLICATIONS IN PEACE DISCOURSE AND GLOBALIZATION

In an address to the Global Forum on Migration and Development, U.N. Secretary General Ban Ki-moon noted:

> It is commonly said we live in a globalized world. Less well understood is that globalization is taking place in stages. We are in its second stage: the Age of Mobility. In its first stage, as flows of capital and goods were liberated, the benefits of globalization flowed primarily to the developed world and its principal trading partners, among them Brazil, China and India. As we enter the newer age of mobility, people will move across borders in ever-greater numbers. In their pursuit of opportunity and a better life, they have the potential to chip away at *the vast inequalities that characterize our time*—and accelerate progress throughout the developing world, (emphasis added).[26]

It would be a grievous error to discuss 21st century peace-keeping strategies without contextualizing that discourse within a broader analysis of globalization. It would add further insult to injury to overlook these vast inequalities, which undermine the importance of the collective global responsibility to address these crises. The development crisis, the global food crisis and the imminent dangers of climate change, are all global issues requiring an immediate interdisciplinary global response. The collective and shared responsibility to mitigate these crises can only be understood within the discourse of an increasingly globalized world. In a discussion of new and strategic approaches to peace education, peacekeeping and peace discourse, adult learners must address the role of peace discourse and peacebuilding within the broader context of globalization.

GLOBAL SEXUAL AND REPRODUCTIVE HEALTH

Tackling the development crisis will invariably be the must difficult of the three crises, simply because at the heart of the development crisis is far more than creating the conditions for economic growth. To understand the significance of the development crisis, adult learners must recognize broader threats to the species, especially threats to human reproduction. Raising awareness about the importance of sexual and reproductive health is of critical importance. In a 2006 report released by the UN at the Global Health Council's 33rd Annual Conference it was noted that:

> 1 in 16 women in sub-Saharan Africa dies from complications of pregnancy and childbirth. This compares with 1 in every 2,800 in highly-developed countries . . . Family planning and obstetric care could radically reduce maternal deaths and injuries . . . The financial resources needed to meet the developing world's sexual and reproductive health needs amount to US$36 billion per year by 2015.[27]

Sexual and reproductive health requires more than simply raising awareness and education. Specifically, when discussing HIV/AIDS Mukherjee (2003) suggests that:

> [the] prevention of HIV infection is often promoted as the only feasible option in resource poor settings despite the existence of drugs to treat it. As recently as 2002, experts argued that prevention should take priority over treatment for AIDS in Africa based on cost effectiveness. However, cost effectiveness analyses fail to take into account the most important reason for implementing widespread HIV treatment? treating sick people. Prevention strategies do nothing to improve the quality or length of life of the millions of people living with HIV. Moreover, the unchecked

spread of HIV is resulting in indirect costs, ranging from orphaning to famine and from stigma to professional burnout, that are damaging already heavily burdened societies.[28]

While education and preventative strategies are certainly important, it is equally important to recognize the existing needs of those already afflicted with both the stigma and the disease. The notion of development is itself contingent on the viability of human reproductivity. Placing emphasis on sexual and reproductive health, safeguards the next generation of producers, laborers, consumers and contributors, in an ever-expanding global economy. Thus, an economically viable global society depends on securing the sexual and reproductive health of every individual throughout the world.

The complexities of the development crisis are further complicated by the lagging global economy. Education, resource allocation, and economic possibilities are all contingent on the capital needed to finance and maintain these structures of development. Without adequate financing, however, it is dangerously unrealistic to assume a blindly utopist stance. The proper and effective allocation of financial resources is essential if we are to maximize the effectiveness of capital investments into combating the development crisis.

THE MISAPPROPRIATION OF HUMANITARIAN AID

The greatest potential to exacerbate the development crisis results as a consequence of the misappropriation of humanitarian aid. One of the greatest misappropriations of humanitarian aid results from its militarization. Therefore, the greatest potential to exacerbate the development crisis results from the attempt to militarize humanitarian aid. In discussing the recent events in Marja, Afghanistan, in a statement from Oxfam, it was noted that "Military-led humanitarian and development activities are driven by donors' political interests and short-term security objectives *and are often ineffective, wasteful and potentially harmful* to Afghans (emphasis added)."[29] There are at least four inherent complications attributed to the attempted militarization of humanitarian aid, which are as follows: (1) the militarization of humanitarian aid is politically-centered not human-centered, (2) the militarization of humanitarian aid diverts financial resources from securing the basic standards of life, (3) the militarization of humanitarian aid undermines the notion of humanitarian aid because it necessitates the destruction of such aid as a basic counterstrategy, and finally, (4) the militarization of humanitarian aid confuses aid workers with military combatants.

CENTEREDNESS AND DEHUMANIZATION

The militarization of humanitarian aid is politically-centered, not human-centered. There are obvious and inherent complications that arise in the attempt to militarize humanitarian aid. In the discourse of peacekeeping and peacebuilding strategies, especially within the larger context of the ensuing development crisis, the militarization of humanitarian aid is fundamentally polemic to the notion of human-centeredness. The notion of human-centeredness is itself substantiated in the belief that the human being and the needs of human beings take ultimate precedence in humanitarian aid and assistance. Furthermore, the very notion of humanitarian aid, by definition, is *humanitarian*, i.e.,

The Andragogy of Peace 29

aid and assistance is focused to better the living conditions of human beings. Insofar, as the motivation of humanitarian aid and assistance is intended to improve the living conditions of human beings, then any and all attempts to militarize humanitarian aid, undermines the essential humanitarian focus of such aid and assistance. In addition to undermining the ultimate motivation in offering humanitarian aid and assistance, the attempted militarization of humanitarian aid, *dehumanizes* all such efforts.

The dehumanization of humanitarian aid results as a consequence of the attempted militarization of such aid. The act of militarizing humanitarian aid is dehumanizing because human beings become pawns in a much larger military strategy. The militarization of humanitarian aid uses such aid as a means rather than an end. The "aid" is merely a ploy in strategically gaining advantage over the opposition, which therefore, undermines and trivializes the significance of such assistance. Attempts to militarize humanitarian aid are further dehumanizing because military strategies must consider possible causalities, which will be assessed and incorporated into the overall strategic objective. For those already war-torn refugees, survivors, and internally displaced persons (IDPs), already devastated by the conflict, the militarization of humanitarian aid, further dehumanizes them by making conditional their aid and assistance. In either case, the attempt to militarize humanitarian aid is politically-centered, not human-centered. This deliberate shift in centeredness is fundamentally an act of dehumanization.

The militarization of humanitarian aid further dehumanizes the population of intended recipients by creating a system of willful confusion, where the distribution of humanitarian aid and assistance is itself a product of militarization. Insofar as humanitarian aid is militarized, strategists willfully attempt to confuse aid and assistance workers with military personnel. This willful confusion knowingly increases the likelihood that nonmilitary personnel will be targeted for attack, which increases the possibility that non-combatants will be killed as a consequence of such militarization. Thus, the deliberate confusion of military personnel with non-combatants as a strategic plan of action dehumanizes non-combatant communities desperately in need of humanitarian assistance.

DIVERSION OF FINANCIAL RESOURCES

The attempt to militarize humanitarian aid diverts financial resources and supplies from intended recipients. For example, international aid and assistance agencies working in Somilia have noted:

> The World Food Programme is conducting an internal investigation in response to allegations that some of its relief supplies are being diverted away from their intended beneficiaries. Britain's Department for International Development (DFID), is "very concerned about allegations of humanitarian food aid being sold for profit in Somalia. Any future contributions to the WFP will be in the light of the findings of the investigation into the alleged misuse of aid."[30]

This misuse of aid, especially food subsidies, drastically undermines global security. Obviously, the attempt to sell food subsidies for profit could lead to an escalation of international violence, by creating a market that generates unregulated capital. The diversion of financial resources and supplies can then be used to subsidize military and paramilitary expansion. The danger in the misappropriation and willful diversion of international subsidies is compounded by an undeniable need for humanitarian aid and assistance. Insofar as a condition for humanitarian aid and assistance exists, there is the potential to garner international financial subsidies. Garnering international financial subsidies for humanitarian aid and assistance can easily be diverted to subsidize military expansion. Thus, it is strategically advantageous for military and paramilitary forces to create a condition wherein international subsidies are contributed, since the contribution of these subsidies creates the necessary conditions needed for military and paramilitary expansion. In an analysis of 21st century peacekeeping strategies then, it is imperative that peacekeepers recognize that the creation of an unstable, hostel, or even genocidal environment actually serves to facilitate and bolster military and paramilitary regimes. In light of the global development crisis, addressed by Secretary General Ban Ki-moon, the crisis is itself hampered by the inextricable relationship between increased development and the import of humanitarian subsidies. It is illogical to assume that one can, on the one hand, speak of remedying the development crisis and, on the other, fail to address the role of humanitarian aid in this process. The development crisis cannot be remedied without the recognition that humanitarian aid and assistance plays an inextricable role in reversing the crisis.

Insofar as international financial subsidies and supplies are diverted from humanitarian aid and assistance and redirected to militarization attempts, the development crisis will only deteriorate. Without specifically addressing the misappropriation of humanitarian aid and assistance, there can be no hope of suppressing the ever-expanding global development crisis. Thus, the crisis is itself, in part, regulated by the efficiency of international financial subsidies to address the needs of those subsidized. The greater the efficiency of these subsidies, i.e., the greater the percentage of donated financial contributions that are used to provide humanitarian aid and assistance, the more likely these subsidies are to contribute both to an improved standard of living and a decrease in the global development crisis. Conversely, however, a decrease in subsidy efficiency suggests a decrease in the standard of living and an escalation of the global development crisis. Recognizing the relationship between the effective use of international financial subsidies and the de-escalation of the global development crisis is an essential aspect in the proper utilization of international financial subsidies. Without this awareness then, attempts to address the global development crisis are bound to fail.

MILITARIZATION OF HUMANITARIAN AID

The inherent problem associated with the deployment of humanitarian aid as a strategic military objective, is that "If that aid is being delivered as part of a military strategy, the counterstrategy is to destroy that aid."[31] Within the scope of strategic military planning and analysis, it is completely justifiable to target humanitarian aid *if* that aid serves a broader military objective. Thus, the very attempt to militarize humanitarian aid, effectively justifies the targeting of such aid on the basis of counter-strategic military objectives. To willfully attempt to militarize humanitarian aid directly undermines the protection such aid would otherwise receive, which places the unnecessary and increased threat that such aid will be targeted for destruction or interception. Insofar as this aid is targeted for destruction or interception, those potential recipients are disadvantaged by the loss of humanitarian aid and assistance. Furthermore, in militarizing humanitarian aid, the process of its militarization effectively compromises the non-combatant immunity of its recipients. If there are grounds to argue for the justification in targeting militarized humanitarian aid, insofar as it is delivered in a larger military strategy, then the benefits of such aid, namely, improving the standard of living and health among devastated populations, becomes precisely the counter strategic opportunity to *decrease* that likelihood. If increasing the standard of living and the health of a given population is of military importance and as such militarized, then the obvious counter-strategy is to exacerbate the alignments of an already devastated population. Thus, the counter-strategic approach to the militarization of humanitarian aid is inherently reactionary. It could not be otherwise. Since the implementation of this counterstrategy increases the likelihood that such aid will be targeted for destruction or intercepted, and since its destruction or interception will result in the collective ailment of the targeted population, then it is imperative that one not provoke such a counter strategic response by refusing to militarize humanitarian aid. In so doing, one undermines the justification of such counter strategic approaches. The loss of this justification should in most cases, but certainly not in all cases, hamper attempts to otherwise target non-militarized humanitarian aid and assistance. Thus, proactive peacekeeping operative measures must be implemented to ensure the non-militarization of humanitarian aid and assistance. Operatively then, peace is at least maintained rather than escalated, since the militarization of humanitarian aid is clearly an act of escalating conflict, which, unfortunately, became a topic of analysis as, "US warships steamed through the Black Sea carrying cargo to help out those beleaguered by the fighting between Georgia and Russia."[32]

In the escalating conflict between Georgia and Russia, the use of U.S. warships undermined, "One of the fundamental principles that relief organizations live by, [simply]: Aid must be directed toward the alleviation of human suffering, without regard for race, creed or nationality, and certainly *without strategic military intent*, (emphasis added).[33] It is the recognition of the *perception* that the militarization of humanitarian aid and assistance is and serves as a direct military threat to the oppositional military forces. Though one may in no sense present a viable threat or intend to present a threat to an oppositional military force, it is the *perception* of the act of militarization that escalates the conflict. Insofar as the conflict is escalated, not only will militarized humanitarian aid be targeted, but non-combatant immunity is fundamentally called into question. Controlling this perception of and avoiding the militarization of humanitarian aid can drastically bolster the peacekeeping process. Thus, recognizing the complications involved in the militarization of humanitarian aid is of the utmost importance if peacekeepers intend to present a viable operational alternative to international conflict escalation.

CONFUSING HUMANITARIAN AID WORKERS WITH MILITARY COMBATANTS

There is a simple and direct connection between the militarization of humanitarian aid and the perception that aid workers are effectively functioning as military personnel, if not combatants. If the deployment of humanitarian aid becomes the operational objective for an overarching military strategy, then those individuals working on behalf of and subordinate to that overarching strategy, themselves become militarized. It is, in effect the militarization of the humanitarian aid worker, or even more grievously stated, the militarization of non-combatants. Since, under normal circumstances, both humanitarian aid workers and non-combatants would generally avoid strategic targeting, to militarize humanitarian aid workers absolves them of their noncombatant immunity. Thus, the militarization of humanitarian aid necessitates the targeting of all members of the humanitarian aid workforce. Furthermore, such militarization, arguably, justifies the direct targeting of all personnel involved in the deployment of militarized humanitarian aid, since their function—within the broader context of a specifically designed military strategy—is itself prone to counter-strategic planning. The obvious counter-strategy would require targeting all participants in the overarching military strategy, and since humanitarian aid workers have effectively been "militarized," their militarization necessarily undermines their non-combatant immunity. "The distribution of aid by the military gives a very difficult impression to the communities and puts the lives of humanitarian workers at risk."[34] Their lives are at risk, precisely because of the militarization of humanitarian aid. Protecting the lives of both humanitarian aid workers and members of the intended population of aid recipients is essential, but is easily compromised by militarization. Reducing this risk is simply at matter of demilitarizing humanitarian aid. Thus, the recognition of non-combatant immunity requires a demilitarized humanitarian aid and assistance program, which can be implemented without bias and solely motivated by attempts to alleviate human suffering. Otherwise, there are theoretical justifications for the willful targeting of humanitarian aid workers functioning within an overarching militarized aid and assistance strategy, since their targeting can be justified within the context of counter-strategic military objectives.

NOTES

1. Turner, Mark, "Security Challenges Prompt Big UN Rethink," *Financial Times (London, England)*, 2003, pp. 09.
2. Renjie, "Business Daily Update: China's Participation Benefits All Global Trading Partners," *Business Daily Update (China)*.
3. Swaminathan, S. Anklesaria Aiyar, "The Economic Times: Globalisation &Amp; Internal Connectivity," *Economic Times, The (Bombay, India)*.
4. "Sub-Saharan Africa Economy: Strategic Rise," Economist Intelligence Unit ViewsWire News Analysis (England), 1.
5. The IMF And Global Coordination, allAfrica.com. (2010).
6. WORLD BANK GROUP, The End of the Third World? M2 Presswire. (2010).
7. Heather, S., (2003), "The Guardian: IMF warns of prolonged conflict jeopardising recovery," *Guardian, The* (London, England).
8. "Think tanks: Another war in Sudan could cost 100 billion dollars," *Deutsche Press-Agentur*. (2010).
9. Gartzke, E. and Q. Li (2003), "War, Peace, and the Invisible Hand: Positive Political Externalities of Economic Globalization." *International Studies Quarterly* 47(4): pp. 582.
10. The Correlates of War Project, Codebook for the Intra-State Wars v.4.0.
11. Thomas Erdbrink Liz, S. (2011), Egypt's revolt stokes fires regionwide, *Washington Post, The* (DC): A1.
12. McClatchy, N. and P. The Washington (2011), Mideast uprisings spur new protests in Iran—VIOLENT CLASHES IN BAHRAIN,

YEMEN Hundreds reported arrested as Iranians defy regime, *Seattle Times, The* (WA): A1.

13. Kaldor, M. (1999) *New Wars and Old Wars: Organized Violence in a Global Era,* Cambridge Polity Press. Duffield, M. (1998) "Postmodern Conflict: Warlords, Post adjustment states and Private Protection," *Civil Wars,* 1 (1): pp. 65–102.

14. Rotberg, Robert I. "When States Fail: Causes and Consequences." Princeton: Princeton University Press, http://www.worldpeacefoundation.org/collapsed.html.

15. Lake, D. A. (2003). "The New Sovereignty in International Relations." *International Studies Review* 5(3): pp. 303–323.

16. Mitch Potter Toronto, S. (2011), "Gadhafi vows to 'cleanse' Libya—Leader lashes out at foreign 'rats' but loses interior minister," *Toronto Star, The* (Ontario, Canada): A6.

17. Harff, B. and T. R. Gurr (1998), "Systematic Early Warning of Humanitarian Emergencies," *Journal of Peace Research* 35(5): pp. 551–579.

18. Ashish Kumar Sen, T. W. T. (2011), Gadhafi uses bloody force in effort to hold grip on Libya—'World is watching,' Clinton warns of alarming violence, *Washington Times, The* (DC): A01.

19. "United Nations: 'We Must Act Now,' Together as One World Community, to Avoid Collapse of Food Security, Says Secretary-General in Hokkaido University Address," *M2 Presswire,* 2008.

20. "Yemen’S Problems Will Not Stay in Yemen, *Yemen Times (Sanaa, Yemen).*

21. John, Cashon, "The Egyptian Revolution and the United States," *Paducah Examiner (KY).*

22. "Uzreport.Com: Food Security as Essential Factor in Sustainable Development of Uzbekistan," *UzReport.com (Uzbekistan).*

23. Etim, Imisim, "This Day (Nigeria)—Aagm: Coalitions Emerging to Tackle Food Crisis," *This Day (Nigeria),* 2008.

24. Tinker, P. B., R. Lal, P. Bullock, C. Valentin, J. Kijne, and H. Fell, "The Environmental Implications of Intensified Land Use in

Developing Countries [and Discussion]," *Philosophical Transactions: Biological Sciences* 352, no. 1356 (1997): pp. 1023–33.

25. "Remarks by the President at the Millennium Development Goals Summit in New York, New York," *allAfrica.com*.

26. "Ban Ki-Moon on Migration in a Globalized World," *Population and Development Review* 33, no. 3 (2007): pp. 647.

27. "Sexual and Reproductive Health Key to Achieving Millennium Development Goals—UN Report Reveals Effectiveness of Ramping up Sexual &Amp; Reproductive Health Service Delivery, Calls for Global Action," *PR Newswire (USA)*, 2006.

28. Mukherjee, J. S., P. E. Farmer, D. Niyizonkiza, L. McCorkle, C. Vanderwarker, P. Teixeira, and Y. Kim, "Tackling Hiv in Resource Poor Countries," *BMJ: British Medical Journal* 327, no. 7423 (2003): pp. 1104.

29. Rod, Nordland, "U.N. Rejects 'Militarization' of Afghan Aid," *New York Times, The (NY)*.

30. "Donor Caution Alarms Aid Workers," *allAfrica.com*, 2009.

31. Rod, Nordland, "U.N. Rejects 'Militarization' of Afghan Aid," *New York Times, The (NY)*.

32. Ken, Hackett, "Military Operations, Aid Organizations Should Be Separate—Commentary," *Daily Messenger (Canandaigua, NY)*, 2008, 5B.

33. Ibid.

34. Rod, Nordland, "U.N. Rejects 'Militarization' of Afghan Aid," *New York Times, The (NY)*.

Chapter Two

Globalization and the Adult Learner

According to John D. Holst (2004) of the University of St. Thomas, "globalization is widely considered to be one of the most important issues facing the field of adult education today." Because of highly integrated communication infrastructures, educational systems are linked through a global network that enables learners and practitioners to exchange information, news, and ideas. For adult education, the challenge presented by globalization is to provide culturally relevant models of education for the global learning community (Kubow, 2009). The global classroom represents the most diverse student body. The ever-changing social and cultural forces create a unique and complex educational environment. The global adult learner by definition is diverse because of the varying perspectives dependent on location, age, gender, ethnicity, and socioeconomic considerations. Uggla (2008) asserts that the *emerging knowledge society* is one that venerates lifelong learning and places its focus on the adult learner. This pedagogical shift from instructor to learner is one that, in terms of globalization, allows for vast interconnectedness between adult learners. Learning becomes a lifelong process with the learner responsible for his or her own experiences. Globalization, then, provides for these learning opportunities to increase exponentially and for the adult learner to experience culturally diverse pedagogy previously unattainable.

The speed with which humans have become a global species has been astonishing (Boucouvalas, 2002). One fear of globalization is that, because of its speed, discourse will become fragmented because of our inability to keep up with the rapidly changing technological global landscape (Boucouvalas, 2002). Moreover, with such an abundance of information that can be accessed globally, the need to "catalyze continuing dialogue while at the same time moving rhetoric to action" is of the utmost importance (Boucouvalas, 2002).

GLOBALIZATION AS INTERNATIONAL ADULT EDUCATION

International adult education has its foundations in the early 1900s with the emergence of the World Association for Adult Education. In addition, with the creation and support of non-governmental organizations (NGOs), international education flourished (Boucouvalas, 2002). The International Council for Adult Education served to further solidify the involvement of the NGOs and, as a result, the ICAE divided the globe into 7 regions in order to better serve in areas of environment, peace, gender equity, indigenous knowledge, and literacy (Boucouvalas, 2002). Much of the international adult educational landscape is dotted with grassroots organizations that aim to address the aforementioned global issues. Adult educators have taken a place among the leaders of these movements and have been able to create a global audience for their causes.

Internationally, adult education consists of practitioners from around the world offering international perspectives on increasingly urgent global issues. Globalization may become problematic however, when the increasing convergence of global perspectives are in opposition with the need for national sovereignty (Boucouvalas, 2002). But, as a tool to educate, "educators of adults have historically been concerned with the empowerment process—giving voice to the oppressed and marginalized, as well as to the more subtly excluded" (Boucouvalas, 2002). Much like Freire (1968), the global community, through education, is charged with recognizing oppression and creating a global discourse aimed at critical consciousness on an international level. The availability of these technological resources and advancements has helped to reshape the adult educational landscape. On a global level, availability has manifest itself in the appearance of online education programs, worldwide blogging and discussion forums, vast social networks, and catalogues upon catalogues of accessible information. Learners are no longer limited by the resources of the local, public, or university library because it has all been uploaded into the internet. A student in West Africa, with only an internet connection, can download textbooks, articles, and podcasts in any subject area. With these advancements in availability, adult educators and instructors have more resources in which to create culturally relevant curriculum and pedagogy and, as a result, provide a better global learning experience.

In order for global adult education to be most effective the "curriculum must be global, technological and contextual"

(King, 2009). The international learning community necessarily utilizes technological advances in an effort to provide accessibility and availability of resources and education to a large adult learner population. Because of the proliferation of global communication, adult learners can experience other cultural ideologies, religions, and value systems. By embracing a global perspective and fostering international adult education as the foundation for tolerance and acceptance, the benefits of a diverse and emerging educated society can be actualized.

PHILOSOPHICAL CONSIDERATIONS OF GLOBALIZATION

As the world becomes increasingly globalized, adult educators must consider new and alternative methods of learning. The adult educator seeks to help facilitate learning instead of the traditional mode of teaching that mandates the instructor as "expert" (Elias and Merriam, 2005). Specifically from a global perspective, adult education exists within the realms of humanistic philosophy and critical theory. These two ideologies best serve to highlight and justify the goals and mission of global adult education and serve to better outline the affects of globalization on the field.

Humanistic adult education centers its focus on the development of the whole learner. In addition, humanistic philosophy maintains that individuals are responsible for "bettering the human state of affairs" (Elias and Merriam, 2005). In a global community, it is this focus on self-improvement that may lead adult learners in search for something more. Once an area is identified that is need of improvement, the adult learner can begin the quest to improve. In terms of globalization, the resources are plentiful. However, in order for the learning to become truly global in nature, the adult learner must seek to transfer his or her learning experience to the global community. By introducing his or her experience to others around the world, the educational experience once confined to the individual can now reach an infinitely larger global society. Instead on the bettering of one, many are affected.

Another philosophical consideration is critical adult education. Globalization widens the point of view for adult learners and may prove as a vehicle to liberating many from political and institutional oppression. Critical theory and humanistic philosophy become linked in the scholarship of Paulo Freire. Freire (1968) posits that the only way to truly become a whole person and experience humanization is to recognize the social forces that are maintaining oppression. He maintains that people can be oppressed over time because they are ignorant of their circumstances and the circumstances of others in the world. The only alternative is to engage in dialectical educational experiences so that the true conditions of the impoverished and oppressed can be revealed.

The implications of globalization are immense. The critical consciousness espoused by Freire can reach massive amounts of the global population. His pedagogy of oppressed peoples can extend outwards as more and more groups of people engage in the "social activity in which individuals communicate through dialogue with others about how they experience reality" (Elias and Merriam, 2005). The foundation of adult education as a learner-centered experience is exemplified through this social connectivity and discourse. Instead of institutionally oppressed individuals from the same region starting a dialogue about their reality, the conversation can exist on an international stage wherein oppressed individuals from around the globe join the discussion. This massive interconnected conversation is made accessible and available because of the rapidly growing technological advances

OPPORTUNITIES PRESENTED BY GLOBALIZATION

The global educational environment is one rife with opportunities for growth. The accessibility of technology and the availability of the internet have put adult learners in a powerful position. No longer must learners depend solely on traditional institutions for education. Online tutorials, universities, chat rooms, blogs, vlogs, and other internet based resources have redefined the roles of teacher and student. Any learner, anywhere in the world can get on a computer and learn something new within minutes. "Lifelong learning, in fact, has become the most important strategy . . . to cope with the challenges from the globalization process by supporting a rapid transition to a knowledge-based economy" (Uggla, 2008). Adult learners need to have the ability to increase their knowledge base in order to compete in the current society. The flexibility of instruction and delivery of educational material has made the adult learner able to experience a wide variety of educational opportunities that were once impossible because of distance and time. Globalization provides the international community with a framework and network that allows for education to be dynamic and portable.

Not only does education become more available to the international community, but the learners are then made available to the international community as well. For example, an adult learner in Asia is able to earn a degree in an online university in the United States. This learner, throughout his or her matriculation, is able to engage in scholarship and discourse with individuals in areas of the world quite unlike his or her own. Upon entering the job market, this individual has the advantage of experiencing an alternate reality. This experience may open up a world of new opportunity, in that he or she may decide to take a job in another part of the world. Globally speaking, the social, economic, and cultural benefits inherent in international learning communities thrive on the flexibility that allows for individuals to broaden their worldviews.

RECOMMENDATIONS FOR PRACTITIONERS

"The recommendation for curriculum developers is to incorporate the cultural knowledge of adult learners so as to not marginalize them from subject matter and thus to foster a more inclusive, democratic learning environment" (Guy, 2009). The democratization of a globalized classroom should reflect the heterogeneity of its diverse student population. In so doing, educators acknowledge and incorporate the possible cultural contributions, which will invariably enrich the global learning experience. In Freire's (1968) discussion of the problem-posing model of education, he notes that educational pedagogy must account for the particular phenomenological experience of each student. Within the newly incorporated globalized classroom, given the enriched learning environment, educators will themselves participate in what Freire (1968) classifies as the "teacher-student" and the "student-teacher" shift, wherein the teacher learns from the phenomenological experiences of her students and the students are able to incorporate their cultural knowledge in the globalized classroom.

Given the technological dependency of any globalized classroom, an easy method for exchanging cultural knowledge is through the use of a discussion board. Students simply have to share a unique cultural experience and relate that experience to the previous post. Gradually, and significantly, students will recognize that despite the vast differences in location and culture, there are a host of similarities between their phenomenological experiences. Thus, the instructor had only to prompt the discussion and allow students to derive shared meaning, despite their cultural differences. As noted by Guy (2009), through the discussion board cultural activity, students were able to incorporate their cultural knowledge and share in an appreciation of their global experience.

Chapter Three

Peace Education and International Diplomacy

Teaching international diplomacy to adult learners can be a daunting task because the topic requires a keen understanding of tolerance and an ability to recognize cultural norms, both of which are contingent on higher order thinking. Learners are continually challenged to mitigate their biases and suspend their disbeliefs in an attempt to learn about the nature of international diplomacy and the peacekeeping process. Teachers, nevertheless, may incorporate a Kantian approach to international diplomacy and a discussion of his ethical concerns, as a pedagogical tool for introducing learners to the requisite concepts needed to address international diplomacy and the peacekeeping process.

Discussing international diplomacy and peacekeeping efforts require learners to use higher order thinking as a means of integrating vast amounts of information, which will be used to characterize the demands of each party involved. In the discussion of higher order thinking, Lewis & Smith (1993) note, "Higher order thinking occurs when a person takes new information and information stored in memory and interrelates and/or rearranges and extends this information to achieve a purpose or find possible answers in perplexing situations" (p. 136). In discussing international diplomacy, learners are required to exercise higher order thinking in their attempts to properly characterize and assess the concerns or grievances of each party. Making such assessments, however, require, first, that they are able to reinterpret relevant bits of information.

Bartlett (1958) suggests that the process of reinterpretation, i.e., a reconfiguration of information, which produces new methods of interpretation, allows the learner to actively process information in distinctively new ways. Learners are presented with a myriad of interpretative possibilities, which pertain to the cultural norms and the practices of political groups—distinct from their own. Learners face the challenge of deciphering stereotypes and caricatures from relevant and substantive cultural differences. Latorre (1985) warns of an inability to properly identify stereotypes, writing, "the distortion produced by focusing on differences, instead of breaking down stereotypes, generously contribute to the perpetuation of cultural misunderstanding, making foreign mores appear more exotic than they really are" (p. 671–672). If learners are to be properly equipped to engage with conceptions like international diplomacy and peacekeeping, they must be able to decipher stereotypes from proper representations.

Take, for example, the sustained irony of Jonathan Swift's (2005) *Modest Proposal*. Certainly, learners will be appalled by Swift's suggestion that, "a young healthy child well nursed, is, at a year old, a most delicious nourishing and wholesome food, whether stewed, roasted, baked, or boiled; and I make no doubt that it will equally serve in a fricasie, or a ragout" (p. 5). There are numerous methods used to interpret Swift's intentions, none of which should include a serious consideration of cannibalism as a means of easing the famine. Such interpretation is no interpretation at all; it takes the text literally, without investigating the possible meaning of the text. Thus, the first step educators can use to incorporate higher order thinking in discussing international diplomacy is to have the learners extrapolate the meaning of the text from its context.

A reconfiguration of information allows learners to uncover otherwise difficult nuances buried within the text. In the example of Swift's *Modest Proposal*, learners can be divided into two groups. Rather than debating the pros and cons of Swift's account, learners can attempt diplomatic negotiations, wherein they persuade members of the other group of the relevance of their claims. The goal is to arrive at an agreement—rather than winning or losing—as is the goal for all instances of international diplomacy. This process is an act of higher order thinking because it challenges members of the group to recognize the concerns of others while reassessing how they initially interpreted the information. In addition to higher order thinking, however, learners will need to incorporate an understanding of tolerance and recognize the multiplicity of interpretations, which will invariably affect attempts toward diplomacy.

UNDERSTANDING TOLERANCE

The *United Nations Educational, Scientific and Cultural Organization* (UNESCO) 1995 Declaration of Principles on Tolerance states:

> 1.1 Tolerance is respect, acceptance and appreciation of the rich diversity of our world's cultures, our forms of expression and ways of being human. It is fostered by knowledge, openness, communication, and freedom of thought, conscience and belief.

Tolerance is harmony in difference. It is not only a moral duty, it is also a political and legal requirement. Tolerance, the virtue that makes peace possible, contributes to the replacement of the culture of war by a culture of peace.

1.2 Tolerance is not concession, condescension or indulgence. Tolerance is, above all, an active attitude prompted by recognition of the universal human rights and fundamental freedoms of others. In no circumstance can it be used to justify infringements of these fundamental values. Tolerance is to be exercised by individuals, groups and States.

1.3 Tolerance is the responsibility that upholds human rights, pluralism (including cultural pluralism), democracy and the rule of law. It involves the rejection of dogmatism and absolutism and affirms the standards set out in international human rights instruments.

1.4 Consistent with respect for human rights, the practice of tolerance does not mean toleration of social injustice or the abandonment or weakening of one's convictions. It means that one is free to adhere to one's own convictions and accepts that others adhere to theirs. It means accepting the fact that human beings, naturally diverse in their appearance, situation, speech, behavior and values, have the right to live in peace and to be as they are. It also means that one's views are not to be imposed on others.

International diplomacy and the peacekeeping process are impossible without a specific understanding of tolerance. As stated in (1.1) of the (UNESCO) declaration, "Tolerance is harmony in difference." Learners must recognize that world views and cultural norms are comprised of different belief systems, which affect each culture to varying degrees. First, recognizing that their particular beliefs differ from others, encourages learners not to measure the degree of difference based on deviations from their own, i.e., learners should not approach the concept of tolerance as an attempt to measure how different "they" are from "us," but also how different we are from them. Addressing the "us," "them" distinction is an important aspect to understanding tolerance, as these binary oppositions often reinforce stereotypes and intolerance. Learners should strive to transition away from these polarizing terms and arrive at inclusive terms like "we" and "all." We are all similar in that we are different. Addressing these differences without judgment, though a difficult task, prepares the learner with the necessary conceptual framework needed to engage in a critical analysis. With respect to the peacekeeping process, learners should understand that polemical terms like "us" and "them" inhibit or suppress attempts toward diplomacy, which, within a political context, tend to encourage violence and acts of evil.

Peacemaking is bolstered by a full understanding of tolerance and an appreciation for the diversity of human life and human experiences. Simply embracing a global understanding of our shared human experience, which is substantiated by our differences, allows learners to recognize that it is our difference that fundamentally make us human. Tolerance, then, within the larger context of an increasingly globalized world requires learners to familiarize themselves with a plurality of cultural, religious and social differences.

Tolerance should not, however, as stipulated in section (1.2) of the (UNESCO) declaration, be articulated in terms of condescension. The act of patronizing others implies or suggests that some cultural norms are better, simply in their difference. This assumption quickly leads to intolerance, insofar as the learner refuses or is unable to recognize that differences in cultural norms and practices does not imply qualitatively better or worse conditions, i.e., it does not follow that because there is a cultural difference, one must be better than the other. Actually, the argument is more tautological. Where there is a cultural difference, there is a cultural difference. The goal is to get the learner to recognize the difference, without ascribing a judgment of value. Though judgments of value may be important to ascribe to cultural differences, such an approach far exceeds the scope of this introductory approach. As suggested by Wainryb et al. (1998), "tolerance emerges as a product of deliberation . . . children and adolescents take into account various parameters of what they are asked to tolerate . . . and the cultural contexts in which people operate and make differentiated judgments" (p. 1153). For an understanding of tolerance to succeed, learners needn't espouse new beliefs as their own. Such demands would surely cripple any attempts toward diplomacy. Rather, the learner should learn to accept a variety of cultural differences, without patronizing one's beliefs. The learner sufficiently capable of recognizing difference without also ascribing qualitative judgments is said to have attained an understanding of tolerance.

TOLERANCE AND HUMAN RIGHTS

Beitz (2001) defines rights broadly as, "Rights of the person refer to life, liberty, and the security of the person; privacy and freedom of movement; ownership of property; freedom of thought, consciousness, and religion . . . and prohibition of slavery, torture, and cruel or degrading punishment" (p. 271). In discussing human rights, adult learners must acknowledge the relevance of both natural and legal rights. On the one hand, natural rights are pre-social and are fundamental to the human experience. These rights do not require the codification of law to be upheld and are universally recognized as applicable to all human beings. Legal rights, on the other hand, are conferred to respective members of the population after the law has been codified. Human rights, then, arise at the convergence of natural and legal rights. Adult learners cannot properly discuss human rights, then, without also discussing both natural and legal rights. Pagden (2003) writes, "Today of course, the definition of 'human rights' has been extended far beyond the limits . . . intended for 'natural rights.' The shift from 'natural' to 'human' reflects a modern unease with the conception of an essentialized 'nature' and, in particular since the death of the natural tradition in Kant, with the idea of the existence of guiding natural principles" (p. 176).

Section 1.3 of the (UNESCO) declaration states, "Tolerance is the responsibility that upholds human rights." There is an inherent responsibility associated with any discussion of rights, namely, the duty a moral agent has to respect or honor a given right. If someone has a right to privacy, for example, others have a duty not to infringe on that person's right. There are those, however, that deny the existence of rights. There are also those that deny the existence of duties. Nevertheless, in discussing the (UNESCO) declaration of tolerance, adult learners cannot properly address the conception of human rights without also addressing these requisite concepts. With respect to the relationship between tolerance and human rights, if it is true that one properly understands the conception of tolerance discussed in the previous section, and one acknowledges the existence of rights as Beitz (2001) has broadly defined, then it must follow that the particular moral agent accepts the duty to uphold the human rights of all persons. It would be a contradiction to both acknowledge that the prohibition of torture is a fundamental right for all human beings and simultaneously assert that it is an acceptable practice under desperate circumstances. Thus, learners must recognize that international diplomacy requires an acceptance of the responsibilities ascribed by a duty to defend and uphold human rights. Diplomats are obligated, then, by their responsibilities and duties to defend human rights. A failure to accept such a responsibility is necessarily a failure in hopes for diplomacy. Unfortunately, however, the failure of international diplomacy is typically the initial stages in the deterioration of the peacekeeping process. Langford (1999) writes, "Among the most difficult challenges facing the UN system of conflict management is the internal disintegration of a state . . . State failure is a complex, multifaceted phenomenon that defies conventional methods of peacekeeping, peacemaking and peacebuilding" (p. 59). As stated in section 1.4 of the (UNESCO) declaration states, "human beings . . . have the right to live in peace and to be as they are." Educators must stress the importance of the peacekeeping process. The peacekeeping process is an integral part of international diplomacy. Without it, there is no use for diplomacy. The goal is to arrive at an agreement, rather than win an argument. Diplomacy, especially with topics as sensitive as torture and state endorsed genocide, require learners to lay aside their biases and embrace a conception of tolerance, only then, can they engage in diplomatic negotiations, upholding the tenants of the peacekeeping process and a fundamental regard for human rights.

KANT'S INFLUENCE ON INTERNATIONAL DIPLOMACY

Immanuel Kant's account of perpetual peace can offer adult learners the possibility of actively engaging with the topic of peacekeeping, on the one hand, and war and diplomacy, as a means of preventing war, on the other. In discussing the peacekeeping process, Kant addresses the impetus to war and our moral responsibility to refrain from war whenever possible. Bourke (1942) writes, "There are two main questions which it is possible to ask about war. The first is, whether it is inevitable; the second, whether it is desirable. The former question is one of fact, the latter one of value" (p. 324). Once learners have sufficiently demonstrated an understanding of tolerance, applying their knowledge of tolerance to political issues offers them the opportunity to analyze how international diplomacy is used as a means to keep the peace. Kant understood the nature of diplomacy and infused his commentary on the politics of war and perpetual peace with an equal account of our moral obligation to refrain from war whenever possible.

In discussing this conception of perpetual peace, however, learners should understand that the state of peace is a difficult state to maintain, i.e., it is easier to destroy than it is to create; it is easier to engage in war than it is to maintain peace. Kant (1983) suggests that, "The state of peace among men living in close proximity is not the natural state; instead the natural state is one of war . . . The state of peace must therefore be *established*, for the suspension of hostilities does not provide the security of peace, and unless this security is pledged by one neighbor to another . . . the latter . . . can treat the former as an enemy" (111). According to Kant, this disposition toward political violence and war is a natural state of affairs, which arises from recognizing an enemy, i.e., "them" as opposed to "us" and eventually results in war. Engaging learners with the difficulties faced by sovereign nations, residing in close proximity, all with varying cultural, religious, and socio-political beliefs, all vying for very limited amount of natural resources, all with access to weapons of mass destruction and the intent on preserving their sovereignty, offers learners a very real sense of the multifaceted difficulties faced in mitigating the impetus to war.

Kant, recognizing these difficulties, argues against the conception that war leads to peace writing, "a war of extermination—where the destruction of both parties along with all rights is the result—would permit perpetual peace to occur only in the vast graveyard of humanity as a whole. Thus, such a war, including all means used to wage it, must be absolutely prohibited" (p. 110). In the rhetoric of preemptive offense as the best defense, Kant clearly denies the consistency of such an argument. The goal of international diplomacy is to prevent war and preserve the peacekeeping process. If, however, our first inclination is to engage in battle and that inclination is shared by our enemies, then what results is an all out war. Moreover, if it is suggested, as is often the case, that preemptive strikes are a necessary means of preserving the peace, then, as Kant suggests, perpetual peace will occur at the expense of the entire human race. Thus, war invariably results in its own destruction, and peace will be attained, but Kant suggests that this may be too great a price to pay. We all have the capacity for either good or evil and in choosing to create weapons as a means of preserving the peace, in so doing, one undermines the very conception of peacekeeping. The complete destruction of the human race is the only logical conclusion if every nation subscribed to the belief that the preservation of peace can be brought about by, as Kant suggested, "a war of extermination." Thus, in discussing international diplomacy, one should encourage adult learners to conceptualize the consequences of "a war of extermination," allowing them to arrive at the conclusion for themselves. Thinking through the various scenarios, discussing the possible consequences of preemptive strikes, should allow learners to, rather skillfully, recognize that the result of a "war of extermination" is the complete annihilation of the human race. In short, then, peace cannot be brought about by war.

For Kant, where there are rights, there is an obligation to recognize those rights through the various duties one has to others. Kant, nevertheless, refutes the idea that one can be burdened with duties without also receiving some degree of rights. He writes, "no one can make a contract to perform some rightful act whereby he has no right but only duties, for in so doing he would cancel it" (1983, p. 74). There is a balance, then, between the obligations one has to others and the rights one attains by obligating others. It is inconsistent to suggest that a moral agent must respect to rights of others and assert that the agent's rights are inconsequential. Such a stance is contradictory.

Since the concepts of rights and duties are fundamental to any investigation of international diplomacy, educators can divide their learners into two groups, one half generating some number of right, and the other half generating corresponding duties to respect those rights. This process allows learners to recognize the relationship between rights and duties through a process of higher order think, since it is their responsibility to generate the relevant relationships. Discussing duties, however, within the scope of international diplomacy and the peacekeeping process, becomes complicated when conceptualizing rights and duties on a state level, i.e., can we effectively discuss rights and duties as one attempts to apply these conceptions to the state? One can imagine that one of the rights generated by a learner may be a right to life, and the teacher may introduce the learners the conception of the sanctity versus the quality of life argument. The question, however, is though a conception of a right to life may hold true with respect to human beings, can such a conception be properly be applied to the state? Interestingly enough, learners will quickly learn that generating the list of rights and duties, with respect to state level politics, is an involved process.

STATE SOVEREIGNTY AND DOMESTIC JURISDICTION

In discussing international diplomacy and the peacekeeping process, one of the most difficult concepts to address is that of state sovereignty. While it is important that nations recognize the sovereignty of other nations, it is precisely within the confines of the state's domestic jurisdiction that abuses of state power can be fashioned as a tool of genocide. A balance, then, must be met between noninterference and intervention once human rights violations have occurred. Tesón (2005) states,

> Force used in defense of fundamental human rights in therefore not a use of force inconsistent with the purposes of the United Nations. State sovereignty makes sense only as a shield for persons to organize themselves freely in political communities. A condition for respecting state sovereignty is, therefore, that sovereignty governments (minimally) respect human rights. Delinquent governments forfeit the protection afforded by article 4(2) (p. 217).

State sovereignty is an essential component of political power without which its government cannot function. Kant also acknowledged the importance of state sovereignty in his discussion of forcible interference. He distinguishes between two possible outcomes. On the one hand, Kant addresses the possibility of a divided state, where the state is essentially split into two warring factions. On the other hand, he addresses the possibility of a state, still unified, where the conflict is undecided. In the example of the former, Kant (1983) suggests that forcible interference would be justified if, "as a result of internal discord, a nation were divided into two and each part, regarding itself as a separate nation, lay claim to the whole; for (since they are in a condition of anarchy) the aid of a nation to one of the parties could not be regarded as interference" (p. 109). The adult learner can then use this conception of justifiable interference to lay claim to governmental interference when instances of genocide and human rights violations are occurring. Thus, it is important for the adult learner to understand that while state sovereignty is an essential component of political power, it is in no sense absolute. The moral consideration for the preservation of human rights and human life outweigh the recognition of a state's sovereignty. Conversely, however, Kant (1983) claims that forcible interference would not be justifiable if, "this internal conflict remains undecided" (p. 109). In contemporary genocide scholarship, many theorists are debating how nations are to interpret the UNGC's acknowledgment of state sovereignty. If genocide is a crime against members of a state's population, within the confines of the state's domestic jurisdiction, which in turn, is protected by state sovereignty, then how is an international community of nations to forcibly intervene on behalf those being systematically exterminated? The United Nations Charter Chapter I, Article 2(7) reads:

> Nothing contained in the present Charter shall authorize the United Nations to intervene in matters which are essentially within the domestic jurisdiction of any state or shall require the Members to submit such matters to settlement under the present Charter; but this principle shall not prejudice the application of enforcement measures under Chapter VII.

In recognizing state sovereignty and the power a state has within its domestic jurisdiction, the UN Charter creates a loophole for any state charged with acts of genocide. Simply put, Article 2(7) of the U.N. Charter recognizes state sovereignty to the extent that the very people the UNGC is set to protect is undermined by Article 2(7), which recognizes domestic jurisdiction over the Articles set forth in the UNGC. Thus, accusations of genocide against state officials have no means of combating their domestic jurisdiction. Kuper (1981) argues to close this loophole in the U.N. Charter Article 2(7) writing,

> [the] central ideological commitment of the United Nations, [is the] respect for the sovereignty of the state. It is *enshrined* in Article 2(7) of the United Nations Charter . . . *the protection of domestic jurisdiction is almost inevitably invoked by any state charged with violating the human rights of its subjects* . . . Human rights are a matter of legitimate international concern. Yet the United Nations remains highly protective of state sovereignty, even where there is overwhelming evidence . . . of widespread murder and genocidal massacre (emphasis added), (Kuper, 1981, p. 181–182).

A Kantian interpretation of the justifications for forcible interference offers scholars the theoretical framework to argue against the absolute recognition of state sovereignty. Genocide is a heinous abuse of political power, which fundamentally undermines the peacekeeping process. States engaged in acts of genocide forfeit their sovereignty insofar as international diplomacy cannot allow for the recognition of state sovereignty over human life and the preservation of peace. In teaching adult learners about international diplomacy, educators must convey a sense of the importance of tolerance and the need to acknowledge the rights and duties of all moral agents. If human rights are being violated and governments are engaged in acts of genocide against members of its population, then, on a Kantian account of forcible interference, nations are justified in their attempts to intervene. Forcible interference, however, is the last resort. Negotiations, and international diplomacy, prior to human rights violations must be recognized as viable tools of the peace keeping process.

Chapter Four

Kantian Cosmopolitism and a League of Nations

Within a brief essay entitled, "Idea for a Universal History from a Cosmopolitan Point of View" Immanuel Kant sets out to investigate the necessary conditions wherein the formation of a league of nations is made possible. His investigation, though brief, is filled with the complexities common to his writings. Kant offers an account of the required conditions, necessary in the actualization of world citizenship. Within his investigation, Kant identifies nine theses essential in the discussion and analysis of the formation of such a league of nations. What is remarkable, with respect to our analysis of peacekeeping efforts in a globalized world, is the lucidity and exactness that Kant employs in his theoretical investigation. Unbeknownst to him, however, was the profound affect and remarkable foresight inherent in his analysis, as his theory would serve to spearhead such a League of Nations.

The purpose of this investigation, then, is to discuss each of the nine theses, attempting to extract a common thread throughout, since the conclusion to which Kant subscribes is nearly alien in the premises of his argument. His genius in the construction of this work is undeniable given the existence of the United

Nation, a League of Nations and a, now, plethora of international legislations criminalizing and regulating war crimes and acts of genocide. Our investigation will also integrate the importance and necessity for an emerging society of adult learners, connected by the technological advancements and innovations of the 21st century, to take the lead in advancing the global community toward a peaceable and interconnected society. Using Kant's required conditions for the formation of a league of nations, it becomes apparent that such a league can be facilitated by the use of learning models that promote dialogic learning environments wherein learners are exposed to the experiences and plights of others in an effort to collaborate and initiate change on a global level. Thus, the power of the proposed League of Nations exists in its insistence on diversity and dependency on international worldviews as a foundation for global justice.

THE NINE THESES OF KANT'S COSMOPOLITANISM

The First Thesis

The first of the nine theses is as follows: *"All natural capacities of a creature are destined to evolve completely to their natural end"* (Kant, 2001, p. 12). Kant begins his investigation with an empirical observation, one that accords with the findings of his time and the sciences of biology and physiology. The tenet of his first thesis rests and is bolstered by a conception of use and purpose, that is to say, a thing evolves and adapts, insofar as it has a use or a purpose for its existence. This purpose propels, if you will, the thing throughout history. For example, and more specifically, the human appendix—once thought to function in the digestion of food or in the facilitation of the immune system, no longer serves a purpose in human beings. Moreover, the organ itself can become infected and lead to fatality. Therefore, biologists have classified this organ as vestigial and while it remains a part of our anatomy, it serves no immediately recognizable purpose. The *telos*, or the purposefulness of such an organ is contrary to the development and *telos* of the organism as a whole. Similarly, the political system is directed toward the purpose of preserving peace and protecting members of its population. Peace serves the purpose of the political structure; its absence complicates the functionality and efficiency of the system. Thus, the structure of the political system is itself contingent on peaceful coexistence.

Kant begins his investigation on these grounds to situate the reader in a familiar discourse, wherein he may find himself comfortable in discussing the topic at hand, for this analysis thus far is rather mundane in its novelty. Kant writes, "Observation of both the outward form and the inward structure of all animals confirm this of them. An organ that is of no use, an arrangement that does not achieve its purpose is a contradiction to the teleological theory of nature" (Kant, 2001, p. 12). Kant is suggesting that Nature, as such, i.e., Nature as a Cosmos, functions through an increase in functionality and efficiency, organs, for example diversify, and Nature increases in its diversity. Hence, though Kant does not express this point himself, one is certainly justified in defending the assertion, based on Kantian grounds, that one of the teleological ends of Nature is an increase in diversity. The antithesis to this increase in diversity, on biological grounds, would be the extinction of a species or the exhaustion of a natural resource. Remember Kant writes, "An organ that is of no use, an arrangement that does not achieve its purpose, are contradictions to the teleological theory of nature." Kant is clearly suggesting that the end, i.e., the *telos*, of Nature is one that accords with progress and discords with uselessness. If diversity accords with the progression of the natural state, insofar as diversity contributes to the overall complexity of the organism, and the resilience necessary for sustaining life, then, diversity must serve as one of the teleological ends to which Kant's argument suggests.

In Kant's first thesis, he explains the strength Nature derives from diversity. The same may be acknowledged for the adult learning atmosphere. The use and purpose of education with respect to adult learners, originates in the Progressive era of education. The Progressive era of education occurred during a time in American history when many areas were becoming urbanized (Elias and Merriam, 2005). The needs to provide a form of education to address the needs of the public were increasing. The increase in foreign-born residents highlighted the need to provide an American education that would teach people how to be citizens. Furthermore, progressive education sought to help society by teaching people how to influence social change. Pragmatism was the philosophical basis for progressive education. As the foundation, pragmatism was used to solve the problems of the human condition. Progressive education, motivated by the work of Charles Darwin, moved away from a focus on theoretical perspectives and, instead, injected scientific method in an effort to ameliorate the human condition (Elias and Merriam, 2005).

Eduard Lindeman, an adult educator, believed that adult learners must acquire knowledge for the purpose of affecting society. More importantly, Lindeman argued for progressive adult education to be the means by which individuals challenged societal norms by demanding change (Lindeman, 1956). Because it is progressive in nature, adult education must adhere to a socially responsible framework that educates for the sake of prescribing change than just merely for its own sake. As a group, adult learners are intrinsically motivated by promotion, societal change, or economy to continue education. In order to achieve this end, the adult learner must exist within an environment that embraces diversity. In Kantian terms, diversity becomes the natural end. Using technology as a tool for a global classroom, adult learners from various regions of the international community can deliberate on any problem plaguing the human condition. The increase in worldview will allow for a broadening of perspective and more fruitful investigation of the function of the "problem" and any proposed solutions. As a result, diversity, as facilitated by the advances in technology, inevitably creates diversity on a global level. Diversity is the tool by which an interconnected, self-directed, socially responsible adult can create and deliberate on ways in which peace can be achieved.

The Second Thesis

The second thesis of Kant's cosmopolitanism is as follows: "*In man (the only rational creature on earth) those natural capacities which are directed to the use of his reason are to be fully developed only within the race, not in the individual*" (Kant, 2001, p. 13). The progression of Kant's argument takes an expected stance in suggesting that reason and its progression is an attribute of the race of men, rather, than of any individual man. First, one should not confuse the term "race" with a particular racial group, to do so would be entirely to misunderstand Kant's argument, for he is not discussing the superiority of any particular race of men. Kant is discussing the relationship between a capacity for reason, solely reserved for humanity, and its correspondence to the race of men as such. For example, the complex function of the human eye fills thousands of pages of medical text and journals. The information within the textbook is an accumulation of data, compiled to illustrate regularity. It is this compilation, this collection of facts gathered by researchers, which, then, refers to the eye in general. Therefore, without years of research and analysis, data collection and observation, a physiological discussion of the function of the eye would be impossible. At best, one would be able to discuss one's own eye but clearly that discussion would be speculative.

Similarly, in the discussion of reason, as such, i.e., not in the discussion of any one person's affinity or capacity for reason, but in the analysis and investigation of reason as a concept, no one man is capable of sufficiently developing his reason to a point of perfection. As our analogy holds, an analysis of the eye requires years of observation and investigation, so too an investigation into the development of reason requires generational research. Note, however, an interesting fact, despite the finitude of the human eye—one's analysis of the eye, in general, can be infinite, i.e., there is an infinite quantity of information that can be written on the eye. Reason is similar. Kant's notion presupposes a contribution or collaboration of information, without which, rational development, on a cosmopolitan scale is impossible. Take for example the linguist who discovers new truths in the analysis of language acquisition. If she embarks on her discoveries and then proceeds to destroy her findings, the overall progression of reason stays the same because her particular knowledge does not contribute to the overall development of reason. Social responsibility and an ethic of educational research with the goal of peace or social growth must have a globally minded audience. It is the contribution of rational minds to a specific topic of investigation, be it scientific, historical, philosophical, literary or other that contributes to the development of reason. This necessity, this requirement for the contributions of others, serves as a system of checks and balances. This discovery, as to the validity of the questions themselves, can only be made possible, in the nexus of a cosmopolitan exchange of information. Otherwise, reason becomes sluggish and dogmatic. To express these points, Kant writes,

> Reason itself does not work instinctively, but requires trail, practice, and instruction in order gradually to progress from one level of insight to another. Therefore a single man would have to live excessively long in order to make full use of all his natural capacities (Kant, 2001, p. 13).

Experience and narrative are necessary components for the advancement of reason. Moreover, they are the vehicles by which others are granted access to alternate realities. Educational researchers toil in their respective universities with the goal of bridging the gap between theory and practice. However, the integrity of any proposed theory or research study relies on its ability to be challenged and duplicated.

> Any supported theory, laden with facts, is only adequate once it has been confronted with several well-developed, alternative theories. Theoretical pluralism then, promotes 'sharper criticism of accepted ideas than does the comparison with a domain of 'facts' which are supposed to sit there independently of theoretical considerations (15).

By cultivating an educational environment that encourages diversity, learners and practioners are able to reap the benefits that result from a culturally sensitive and relevant worldview. Since experience can shape outlook, it is imperative that researchers and learners have a forum where diversity is honored. The global experience facilitated by deliberation necessarily supports and promotes an atmosphere that look for international contributions and solutions to problems of the human condition. "We must learn to be vulnerable enough to allow the realities of others to edge themselves into our consciousness" (Delpit, 2006).

The Third Thesis

The third thesis of Kant's cosmopolitanism is as follows: *"Nature has willed that man should, by himself, produce everything that goes beyond mechanical ordering of his animal existence, and that he should partake of no other happiness or perfection than that which he himself, independently of instinct . . . has created* (Kant, 2001, p. 13). Unlike the prior two theses, the third thesis of Kant's cosmopolitanism transcends the level of the here and now or a given account of the existence of rational development to discuss our responsibility to future generations. In the third thesis, Kant begins by illustrating that man owes his intellectual progression to no other force but himself, "he alone should have credit and should have only himself to thank" (Kant, 2001, p. 15).

Kant then transitions into a conception of work and toil. He writes, "he should work himself upward so as to make himself" (Kant, 2001, p. 15). If man is to thank none but himself for his achievements, and as we have seen Nature is teleological in its unfolding, then (1) man's place in Nature is part of the unfolding or the historical progression of Nature but more profoundly (2) man's achievements manifest independent to Nature's teleological end. That is to say, our ability to find happiness, or love, or peace—functions separately though simultaneously with the teleological progression of Nature. To make this point clearer, our happiness and well-being are superfluous to the Natural ordering of things. Attributing feelings of care and concern to Nature, would be a gross attribution of anthropomorphism. It is for this reason then, that the existence of happiness and love should be noted, for such an existence is made possible only through the toil of is manifestation. Nature does not create happiness, man does. Nature does not bring about love, we do. Most importantly, Nature is not the source of peace, we are.

Peace then, is a construct of our cognitive ability. We are the kinds of beings capable of creating conflict, but we are equally the kinds of beings capable of finding resolutions to our conflicts. Resolutions unfold as a consequence of our desire to attain balance and equilibrium in our systems of belief. Differing systems of belief are able to reconcile with each other through a deliberative and global worldview that promotes and values the contributions made by a diverse society. It is in these various systems that our desire to find peace governs the methodology of conflict resolution. Thus, it is impossible to conceive of a system of conflict resolution that functions independent to an overarching recognition of the importance of peace and collective and cooperative action. Adult education is the means by which this cooperation is cultivated. Conflict resolution unfolds as we "toil," which will be discussed shortly, or labor for peace. The resolution of our conflict is an instance of peace, which requires that potential conflict resolutionist have thorough training and understanding in the theoretical aspects of peacekeeping.

Now in the third thesis, Kant makes an even more impressive transition. He suggests that since we are to be praised for our effort and toil, the question arises as to the nature of our *telos*. As finite beings, our toil and effort cannot simply be of ourselves, as we are necessarily social animals. Our toil is for, though not readily apparent, the happiness of future generations. Kant writes,

> It remains strange that the earlier generations appear to carry through their toilsome labor only for the sake of the later, to prepare for them a foundation on which the later generations could erect the higher edifice *which was Nature's goal*, and yet that only the latest generations should have the good fortune to inhabit the building on which a long line of their ancestors had (unintentionally) labored without being permitted to partake of the fortune they had prepared (emphasis added), (Kant, 2001, p. 15).

For example, during the civil rights movement of the late 19th and early 20th century, African-Americans fought and died for policies to which they were themselves unaccounted. Because of their toil, future generations would reap the benefits they were not afforded. Thus, future generations receive benefits of past labor. Properly stated then, there is an obligation to future generations, which must be accepted by the current generation. That he was able to specifically identify an obligation to future generations allows the analysis to transition easily into the fourth thesis.

In order for society to adapt to the changes ushered by globalization and technology, social critique and change are of utmost importance. Some of the most prolific social change movements began with education as a necessary component. Bergevin (1967) viewed social change as the means by which individuals become active participants in the social order. Moreover, these "social members" were responsible for preserving and enhancing the democratic ideals espoused by their forefathers. By understanding the history and role of social change in education, adult learners will be better able to make lasting change in the global community. This change, however, as we have seen, is often directed toward future generations.

The highest form of education is the type that opens outward into the world. It is important that education serve a purpose, community, and future generations. The responsibility of the educator and the educated is to free those that cannot free themselves. Freire (1968) has written that once the oppressed are educated and freed from bondage, it is vital that the knowledge gained be shared. Without a greater purpose, education for its own sake exists in a narrow reality affecting nothing. Societies have historically progressed when great thinkers have challenged a commonly held societal belief. These great men and women have reached the highest levels of education because their efforts have led to societal, national, and sometimes global changes that may not have occurred during their own lifetimes. Social change will never become an idea of the past because to abandon it is to stagnate as a people, as a culture.

The Fourth Thesis

The fourth thesis of Kant's cosmopolitanism is as follows: *"The means employed by Nature to bring about the development of all the capabilities of men is their antagonism in society, so far as this is, in the end, the cause of a lawful order among men* (Kant, 2001, p. 15). Once the hurdle of the third thesis is bridged, the fourth thesis follows nicely from the findings in the third. Man must opt out of the barbarism of, to use a Hobbesian phrase, a "state of nature" to enter into a social contract with other members of humanity so that particular men and women may enjoy an individual pursuit of happiness. Paulo Freire, a critical theorist, believes that it is vital to destroy any system in which there exists an oppressor and oppressed. Moreover, although it is obvious that the oppressed are enslaved by the system, so too is the oppressor. The solution, according to Freire, is through education. The adult learner seeks, through education, to free both members of an oppressive society be it economic enslavement, social enslavement, or ideological enslavement. Within this conception of man's sociability, however, Kant is able to bring to the forefront an interesting conception, namely, that "man wishes concord; but Nature knows better what is good for the race; she wills discord" (Kant, 2001, p. 16). Of importance to our investigation, is the assertion that there exist an opposition between the teleological end of Nature and that of man. Man seeks happiness, love, comfort, Nature, on the other hand seeks, discord predation and strife. However, what is evident from Kant's writings is that Nature seeks this end so that the net effect of man's suffering leads to his will to survive. For Kant, it is only through suffering and overcoming the worst of things that we can alleviate our pains and enjoy the best of things. By engaging in thoughtful dialogue resulting from a shared experience between self and others, learners will be able to re-create their knowledge and environment (Freire, 1968). This ability to create and seek out other opportunities besides those available will help adult learners to better navigate the diverse international community. To illustrate this conception Kant writes, "Nature wills that he should be plunged from sloth and passive contentment into labor and trouble, in order that he may find *means* of extricating himself from them" (emphasis added), (Kant, 2001, p. 16). In this sense, the adult learner uses continuing education as the means of removing him or herself from a state of sloth or passivity. Continuing education becomes the means by which adult learners navigate the educational landscape in an effort to reach some level of advancement. The means is at stake, not the struggle or the suffering. The means of one's struggle out of suffering serves as a generalized template out of similar circumstances. By using the internet and others means of social networking, adult learners are able to connect with others internationally and share stories of struggle. Similar to our previous discussion of the eye, the knowledge of overcoming a particular struggle does not develop within one's lifetime but over the course of many years—possibly generations. Technology and globalized education further the impact of the struggle as it serves as a template for not only the microcosm but the global community. For example, during American slavery abolitionist organizations often published narrative accounts "written" by former or fugitive slaves. The runaway slaves would dictate their stories of bondage and freedom while white abolitionists transcribed each word. If these narratives were then placed in a vault, then their lasting impact would have been lost. However, these slave narratives served a greater purpose once published and promoted to the public at large. The plight of the American slave, "written" by the American slave could now be consumed by society. This sharing of experience helped to introduce the struggle of the American slave to a society that either ignored the atrocities of slavery or remained ignorant. It can be argued that some white Americans might have joined the antislavery movement after having read a slave narrative. Adult educations seeks to increase this sharing of experience by advocating for a globally minded curriculum that allows for its diversity to be its strength.

Similarly, in a global community, individuals can connect via the internet. Much of the discord and divisive behavior in the world results from a lack of understanding. Often, one group of people will make false assumptions about another group and this can lead to terrible outcomes. However, by utilizing technology, people are granted exposure to others in an environment that can foster acceptance over tolerance. For instance, in an adult education course, learners are required to engage in international discussion forums where the goal is to share personal histories and experience. Over time it will become evident that, although the specifics of the human experience differ, the inherent emotions and ambitions are similar. Learners in one corner of the world do not have to belong to the same culture to value family, education, or human rights. However different opinions may be, the ability to discuss these similarities and differences can lead to new insights and new realities.

For example, technological advances have led to a massive migration from agricultural regions into cities, which in turn led to an underdevelopment of agricultural resources and over development of machinery, which in turn led to socially constructed poverty and famine. However, it is only through an experience of poverty and famine that we, as a society, are able to formulate measures to safeguard from its reoccurrence. These measures are the means to which Kant refers. Our knowledge of the existence of poverty informs our attempts to eradicate its occurrence. Merely knowing of the existence of struggle, poverty, and famine is not enough in a socially minded ideology. The adult learner in a global classroom becomes witness to these realities and has a social responsibility to take action in order to increase awareness and encourage activism. Poverty is not unique or exclusive to one group of people, rather it is a truth acknowledged globally. Since this is the case, its eradication is the responsibility of a global community. In order to mobilize others in the quest to end poverty, the utilization of technology is vital. Social networking sites provide fertile ground for like-minded people to connect, plan, and take action. Instead of affecting change locally, activists can affect change globally.

The Fifth Thesis

The fifth thesis of Kant's cosmopolitanism is as follows: "*The greatest problem for the human race, to the solution of which Nature drives man, is the achievement of a universal civic society which administers law among men*" (Kant, 2001, p. 16). If it is agreed that men are social creatures, and as such seek their own happiness, then there will inevitably be conflicts in the pursuit of happiness, in that the pursuit of any one individual's happiness may entail preventing others from the pursuit of their happiness. In a very succinct sentence Kant writes,

> a society in which freedom under external laws is associated in the highest degree with irresistible power, i.e., a perfectly just civic constitution, is the highest problem Nature assigns to the human race; for Nature can achieve her other purposes for mankind only upon the solution and completion of this assignment (Kant, 2001, p. 16).

It is, then, according to Kant, our greatest problem and consequently, if one follows his argument, our greatest achievement, to balance individual freedom with a lawful society. Granted, Kant is not speaking of absolute freedom, as such a claim results in the loss of freedom altogether. Rather, Kant is arguing that the greatest of all challenges for human societies is the attempt to balance the freedoms of the individual citizen with the laws that govern the citizenry. The vast majority of the citizenry will obey, a remainder will break laws only insofar as they furnish no ill effect to others, and a small percentage will out rightly defy the law. The balancing act, which continues today, is the attempt to regulate the conduct of the smallest portions of society, i.e., those who deliberately break the law with the intentions of inflicting harm to others. Overcoming this difficulty would be our greatest achievement. By incorporating and embracing diversity, adult learners are better able to understand their experiences and the experiences of others in an effort to initiate peace. When adult learners cannot identify with others, they merely *view* another's circumstances as an onlooker. On the other hand, when individuals are vested in an educational community in which they are validated, they are able to *see* the others for who they really are (Tyack, 1976). This distinction is important, as it is reminiscent of the contrast between empathy and sympathy. What is implied in "way of seeing" is the agency of the seer. They are the eyewitnesses, so to speak. The information is being "seen" therefore, it has a subjective point of view. It also seems to imply participation and experience with whatever is being seen. The saying, "In my eyes . . ." fits this example. When adult learners feel a connection to another, they are better able to relate and think critically about what is happening the world around them. This similarity of experience can best occur for the diverse student in that it grants them access and validates their experience as one of the group (Tyack, 1976). Technological advancements have allowed for exponential shared experience with the international community.

However, "ways of viewing" connotes something different for adult learners. To view something more aptly describes watching rather than experiencing. It seems a passive action and lends it self to the less emotional "in my point of view," almost as if it is describing a location rather than an emotion. The *seer* is the empathizer and the *viewer* is the sympathizer. The *seer* is subjective, while the *viewer* is objective. Adult education based in a liberal and critical ideology, allows learners to be active participants in their learning. Instead of reading the experience of someone that you may sympathize with but never truly understand, a discursive adult education program may allow for empathy and true understanding to take place when learners acknowledge and promote their differences, not to make distinctions, but to broaden a greater understanding of others. For example, an earthquake survivor in Haiti can connect with an earthquake survivor in Japan and create meaningful dialogue about the shared experience and, as a result, educate others not directly affected by a natural disaster. Moreover, the individuals may use the found connection of experience to help advocate change in their respective communities.

Unfortunately, the power dynamic does not allow for this organic type of education to transpire (Delpit, 2006). Adult education must occur in an environment that promotes differences as the tool to liberate learners' minds and deepen their understanding of themselves and others. By refusing to accept the world as it is, the critical theorist demands that global citizens take off the blindfold and commit to a recreation of experience and reality. This can only be achieved through a problem solving approach that provides for extensive constructive conversation. Being able to partake in an international discussion will inevitably lead to action taken by socially minded individuals linked by similarity of experience or exposure to the experience of others.

The Sixth Thesis

The sixth thesis of Kant's cosmopolitanism is as follows: "*Man is an animal which, if it lives among others of its kind, requires a master*" (Kant, 2001, p. 17). Kant is possibly purposefully ambiguous as to what or who constitutes this "master." It could be a person or a group of people; it could be the law or it could be God. There is no indication as to the nature of the "master." The master to whom Kant refers cannot be an individual man, as such a suggestion runs counter to his second thesis. The master to whom Kant refers cannot be God, as such a suggestion runs counter to his third thesis, which suggests that (1) since the fifth thesis was a discussion of the law and (2) society must seek to balance the freedoms of the citizenry under the purview of the law, then it follows that Kant must be referring to the law or some sense of universal law with respect to his reference. Such an interpretation also coincides with his deontological ethic and his articulation of the Categorical Imperative. Again, the law banning slavery arose from the means—technological, economic and moral, which displaced slavery as an unnecessary, cost exhaustive and immoral practice—it is the means that brought about the legislation and not the legislation that brought about the means. Hence, the law must prevent regression. If the end of our "toil" and the greatest possible achievement of human beings results in our peaceful coexistence, the law must ensure that as we progress through time we do not return to a former state of depravity. Though the barbarity of the coliseums were at one time acceptable, it should never be the case that we return to a time in which those actions are acceptable.

Because laws are socially constructed, it is vital to value the process of lawmaking over the actual law. So the value of the law is in its ability to be contextualized, amended, or repealed given thoughtful deliberation by a diverse governing body. Although crimes against the human condition are inevitable, the process by which the global community seeks to eradicate injustice is of utmost importance. This process is facilitated primarily through education. Adult learners search for opportunities to initiate social change in an attempt to improve the human condition.

The Seventh Thesis

The seventh thesis of Kant's cosmopolitanism is as follows: "*The problem of establishing a perfect civic constitution is dependent upon the problem of a lawful external relation among states*" (Kant, 2001, p. 18). The seventh thesis of Kant's cosmopolitanism transitions perfectly from the last six. Kant was able to derive the conception of a League of Nations (soon to be discussed) from the prior six theses despite the skepticisms of his contemporaries. Kant is almost apologetic for even suggesting the possibility for the existence of such a conception. He writes, "However fantastical this idea may seem—and it was laughed at as fanatical by Abbé de St. Pierre and Rousseau . . ." (Kant, 2001, p. 19). Clearly, it was not believed that in a few brief pages, of which this analysis focuses, Kant was able to justify such an alien conception as a League of Nations, but despite its brevity, Kant is able to incorporate and validate such globalism, in a time when the mere suggestion of which seemed "fanatical." Kant writes, "In a league of nations, even the smallest state could expect security and justice, not from its own power and by its own decrees, but only from the great league of nations . . . from a united power acting according to the decisions reached under the laws of their united will" (Kant, 2001, p. 19). The conception of structuring an international political system, wherein even the weakest of states can "expect security and justice," itself contingent on the recognition of the role of Nature in the process of our pursuit for peace, was generations ahead of its time.

The peacekeepers of tomorrow are the learners of today. Adult learners seek to derive meaning, change, and happiness from solving the problems they encounter. On a global scale, the adult learners' ambitions are those of social justice stemming from culturally relevant dialogue facilitated by technology. The "League of Nations" becomes a reality when men and women from diverse social, economic, and ethnic backgrounds deliberate on the problems facing the world. This international discourse is made possible by an acknowledgment of the contributions each nation can make in the governance of the international community. However, such a league does not exist without some measure of cooperation and acceptance. In order for a League of Nations to be successful it must function with a framework that welcomes and encourages diversity of experience. As a learning model, adult education promotes an atmosphere that necessitates discourse in an attempt to solve real world problems and initiate a call to action. By adhering to a global perspective, adult learners experience a far richer learning environment that uses the intellect and experience of many to tackle problems of the human condition. Thus, an international adult learning community is in fact a microcosmic example of a league of nations in that it depends on diversity and deliberation as tools for progress.

The Eighth Thesis

The eighth thesis of Kant's cosmopolitanism is as follows: *"The history of mankind can be seen . . . as the realization of Nature's secret plan to bring forth a perfectly constituted state and the only condition in which the capacities of mankind can be fully developed, and also bring forth that external relation among states which is perfectly adequate to this end"* (Kant, 2001, p.

21). Half of Kant's directive has been accomplished, i.e., we live in a time where we can benefit from Kant's theory of universal history (thesis three) insofar as the United Nations is a fact of the matter. This leaves the other half of Kant's eighth thesis, namely, the formation of a perfectly constituted state. Since Kant has proven himself, someone or some group of people should assume the responsibility of investigating the coherence of such a claim. Is it valid to suggest that the possibility of such a state? It seemed as though we, as a global society, despite the atrocities of the world, were on tract to fulfilling what seems to be Kant's utopist conception of a world society, insofar as the formation of the United Nations, partly due to the atrocities of World War II dramatically elevated the status of our overall sense of morality—through the acceptance of a shared responsibility. However, if the United Nations it to actually possess the power to which Kant refers, subsidiary governments would have to ratify their respective constitutions in such a manner as to subordinate its laws to the laws of the United Nations, or some such international third party. As was evident in the a previous presidential debate President Bush scoffed at the suggestion,

> In our first debate [Sen. Kerry] proposed America pass a global test. In order to defend ourselves, we'd have to get international approval. That's one of the major differences we have about defending our country. I'll work with allies. I'll work with friends. We'll continue to build strong coalitions. But I will never turn over our national- security decisions to leaders of other countries. We'll be resolute, we'll be strong, and we'll wage a comprehensive war against the terrorists.[1]

It is interesting to take account of the comprehensive loss of human life that has resulted from our invasion. Contrast Bush's claim with the Secretary-General Annan's caution, "I hope we do not see another Iraq-type operation for a long time—without UN approval and much broader support from the international community . . . I have indicated it was not in conformity with the UN charter from our point of view, from the charter point of view, it was illegal."[2]

The United Nations serves as a prime example of what a diverse, discursive, problem-centered approach to education looks like. The strength of the UN lies not in the power of individual countries but in the varied perspective each offers. As a whole, each country is operating under a shared vision which draws upon the experiences and knowledge of many cultures. For the adult learning community, the UN can provide the template by which emergent peacekeepers model their own andragogy. Contrary to the remarks made by former President Bush, international law, as set forth by the United Nations, would not subordinate the importance of the laws of the United States since the US would have been part of the process of creating the international law. If the United States is present when international laws are created, then the law will inherently speak to the needs and values of the American people.

The Ninth Thesis

In the most pressing and directed thesis, Kant's ninth and final thesis on cosmopolitanism is as follows: *"A philosophical attempt to work out a universal history according to a nature plan directed to achieving the civic union of the human race must be regarded as possible and, indeed, as contributing to this end of Nature"* (Kant, 2001, p. 23). Arguably, Kant realizes that speculation as to the validity of such an investigation as, "bringing forth a perfectly constituted state" may seem implausible and fanciful. Nevertheless, the second half of thesis eight was deemed fanciful by his peers and Kant's analysis has proven itself as consistent and true. In the ninth thesis, Kant gives a glimmer of hope, "Even if we are too blind to see the secret mechanism of its workings, this Idea may still serve as a guiding thread for presenting as a system, at least in broad outlines what would otherwise be a planless conglomeration of actions" (Kant, 2001, p. 24).

Although the existence of a "perfectly constituted state" may be a stretch for some, the goal of attainment is still noble. In the effort to achieve a perfect state, the global community will learn through experience, trial, and error. Together, these experiences will form a global narrative that will serve future generations as a template and universal history from which mistakes can be avoided. For adult learners, social justice is not a finite quest but an ongoing journey that remains subject to context, technology, and time. As the global community changes, so too do technological advances. More pressing present day dilemmas replace problems of the previous decade. The continual attempt to solve social ills will inevitably initiate fruitful deliberation that may prove socially relevant. Thus, an andragogy of peace is an essential step in the contemporary education of adult learners.

NOTES

1. Murphy, Jarrett. "Text of Bush-Kerry Debate III (3)." CBS News, http://www.cbsnews.com/stories/2004/10/13/politics/main649097.shtml.
2. Editor, BBC News Staff. "Iraq War Illegal, Says Annan." BBC News, http://news.bbc.co.uk/2/hi/middle_east/3661134.stm.

References

Bartlett, F.C. (1958). *Thinking: An Experimental and Social Study.* London: Allen & Unwin.

Beitz, C.R., (2001). Human Rights as a Common Concern, *The American Political Science Review*, Vol. 95, No. 2 (Jun.), pp. 269–282.

Bergevin, P. (1967). *A philosophy for adult education.* New York: Seabury.

Boucouvalas, M. (2002). International adult education: past, present, and into the future. *Adult Learning.* Vol. 13 (4).

Bourke, J. (1942). Kant's Doctrine of "Perpetual Peace" *Philosophy*, Vol. 17, No. 68 (Nov.), pp. 324–333.

Cuban, L. (1984). Policy and Research Dilemmas in the Teaching of Reasoning: Unplanned Designs. *Review of Educational Research*, 54, pp. 655–681.

Delpit, Lisa. (2006). Other People's Children: Cultural Conflict in the Classroom. New York: The New Press. pp. 223.

Duffield, M. (1998) "Postmodern Conflict: Warlords, Post adjustment states and Private Protection," *Civil Wars*, 1 (1): pp. 65–102.

Elias, J., & Merriam, S. (2005). *Philosophical foundations of adult education* (3rd ed.) Malabar, FL: Krieger Publishing.

Freire, Paulo. (1968) *Pedagogy of the oppressed*. New York, NY: Continuum.

Guy, T. (2009). Curriculum development for adult learners in the global community. Malabar, FL: Krieger Publishing.

Harff, B. and T. R. Gurr (1998). "Systematic Early Warning of Humanitarian Emergencies." Journal of Peace Research 35(5): pp. 551–579.

Holst, J. D. (2004). Globalization and education within two revolutionary organizations in the United States of America: a gramscian analysis. *Adult Education Quarterly* Vol. 55 (1).

Kaldor, M. (1999) New Wars and Old Wars: Organized Violence in a Global Era, Cambridge Polity Press.

Kant, I. (1983). *Perpetual Peace and Other Essays*. trans. Ted Humphrey. Indianapolis: Hackett Publishing Company.

———. (1998). *Religion within the Boundaries of Mere Reason*. New York: Cambridge University Press.

———. (2001). *Groundwork of the Metaphysics of Morals*. New York: Cambridge University Press.

King, K. (2009). Curriculum development for adult learners in the global community. Malabar, FL: Krieger Publishing.

Kubow, P. K. (2009). Globalization, diversity, and the search for culturally relevant models for adult education. *International Education*. Vol. 39 (1).

Kuper, L. (1981). *Genocide: Its Political Use in the Twentieth Century*. New Haven: Yale University Press.

Lake, D. A. (2003). "The New Sovereignty in International Relations." International Studies Review 5(3): pp. 303–323.

Langford, T. (1999). Things Fall Apart: State Failure and the Politics of Intervention, *International Studies Review*, Vol. 1, No. 1 (Spring), pp. 59–79.

Latorre, G. (1985). Teaching "Culture," Culture and Culture. *Hispania*, Vol. 68, No. 3 (Sep) pp. 671–673.

Lewis, A. & Smith, D. (1993) Defining Higher Order Thinking, *Theory into Practice*, Vol. 32, No. 3, Teaching for Higher Order Thinking (Summer), pp. 131–137.

Lindeman, E. (1956). *The democratic man: selected writings of Eduard Lindeman*. Edited by Robert Glessner. Boston: Beacon Press.

Mukherjee, J. S., P. E. Farmer, D. Niyizonkiza, L. McCorkle, C. Vanderwarker, P. Teixeira, and Y. Kim.

Nickerson, D.S., Perkins, D.N. & Smith, E.E. (1985). *The Teaching of Thinking*. Hillsdale, NJ: Erlbaum.

Pagden, A. (2003). Human Rights, Natural Rights, and Europe's Imperial Legacy, *Political Theory*, Vol. 31, No. 2 (Apr.) pp. 171–199.

Swift, J. (2005). *A Modest Proposal*. San Diego: Icon Group International, Inc.

Tesón, F. R. (2005). *Humanitarian intervention: an inquiry into law and morality*. Dobbs Ferry, N.Y.: Transnational.

Tinker, P. B., R. Lal, P. Bullock, C. Valentin, J. Kijne, and H. Fell. "The Environmental Implications of Intensified Land Use in Developing Countries [and Discussion]." Philosophical Transactions: Biological Sciences 352, no. 1356 (1997): pp. 1023–33.

Tyack, David B. (1976). *Ways of seeing: an essay on the history of compulsory schooling*. Harvard Educational Review. 46, (3), pp. 355–389.

Tzu, L. (1993). *Tao Te Ching*, trans. Stephen Addiss and Stanley Lombardo. Indianapolis: Hackett Publishing Company.

Wainryb, C., Shaw, L.A., & Maianu, C. (1998). Tolerance and Intolerance: Children's and Adolescents' Judgments of Dissenting Beliefs, Speech, Persons, and Conduct, *Child Development*, Vol. 69, No. 6 (Dec.), pp. 1541–1555.

Uggla, B. K. (2008). Who is the lifelong learner? Globalization, lifelong learning, and hermeneutics. Studies in Philosophical Education. Vol. 27 (4).